This book is to be returned on or before
the last date stamped below.

115099

Orders: Please contact How2become Ltd, Suite 2, 50 Churchill Square Business Centre, Kings Hill, Kent ME19 4YU.

Telephone: (44) 0845 643 1299 - Lines are open Monday to Friday 9am until 5pm. Fax: (44) 01732 525965. You can also order via the e mail address info@how2become.co.uk.

ISBN: 978-1-907558-04-7

First published 2010

Typeset for How2become Ltd by Good Golly Design, Canada, goodgolly.ca

Printed in Great Britain for How2become Ltd by Bell & Bain Ltd, 303 Burnfield Road, Thornliebank, Glasgow G46 7UQ.

CONTENTS

INTRODUCTION

Dear Sir,

Thank you for purchasing your new guide, How2become a Royal Marines Commando: The Insider's Guide.

As you are probably already aware, Royal Marines are a unique breed of people who are both professional and extremely skilled in everything they do. They have deservedly earned the reputation for being a formidable fighting force and are very well respected by other Armed Forces around the globe.

Royal Marines are a maritime-focused, amphibious, highly specialised light infantry force who are capable of deploying at short notice anywhere in the world. As the United Kingdom Armed Forces' specialists in cold weather warfare, Royal Marines provide lead element expertise in the NATO Northern Flank and are optimised for high altitude operations, with jungle training still carried out when deployments allows.

The selection process for becoming a Royal Marines Commando is extremely tough. There is a very good reason why

the Corp has used the strap line "99.9% need not apply" in a recruitment campaign. It is aimed at attracting the right type of person who has the potential to join this elite unit. Being a Royal Marines Commando is about having the right attitude, the right level of professionalism and also the right level of physical and mental fitness.

The purpose of this guide is to prepare you for every element of selection, from interview skills through to physical fitness. Read the guide carefully and follow the tips that have been provided by the author very carefully. During the selection process, focus on the word 'perseverance'. Always look to improve your weaker areas and use an action plan that is focused on improving your abilities. Aim for 100% at all times.

Best wishes,

The how2become team

The How2become team

PREFACE

By Author Richard McMunn

Over the years I have known, and worked with, many Royal Marines. I have never met one who was unprofessional, disorganised or unfit. They are, in my opinion, an unbelievable type of person.

The first time I came across Royal Marines was during my time onboard HMS Invincible. I was working as an Aircraft Engineer on 800 Naval Air Squadron, living in mess number 2 Bravo. The mess (living quarters) was situated directly above 3 Bravo, which was the home and living quarters of the Royal Marines unit tasked with ship security. I recall that they were a twelve-man team who generally kept themselves to themselves. One thing I do remember about them was their training sessions, both in the gym and up on the flight deck. I was a keen weight trainer and spent five or six hours per week down the gym, which was located right at the bottom deck of the ship. Even though I trained very hard, I could never quite understand how the Royal Marines could always lift twice as much as me, and work out for twice as long! Apart from being twice the size of me, and I'm six feet tall,

they had this strange state of mind. Basically, nothing fazed them. They had this belief that they could achieve what they wanted, regardless of how tough the task or obstacles were. Their training sessions were very intense and they totally focused on their workouts. They wanted to be at their best and be fully prepared for every eventuality.

The second time I came into contact with Royal Marines was during my career in the Fire Service. I joined Kent Fire Brigade at the age of 21 after serving four years in the Royal Navy. On my Fire Service recruit course there were a couple of ex-Commandos. I knew they were ex-Commandos the minute I saw them. Again, they kept themselves to themselves and just got on with the job, always carrying out their work to the best of their ability. Their professionalism was inspiring and they were extremely organised in everything they did.

I also served on the same watch as an ex-Commando during my time in charge of Green Watch at Maidstone Fire Station. He spent just about all of his spare time in the gym, even though he was in his forties! His level of fitness was astounding, and his resting heartbeat was usually around the 40 mark. When we attended fires and other such emergency incidents I was always glad to have him on the back of the fire engine. Even during some horrendous fires, car accidents and chemical incidents he was always as calm as a cucumber. Nothing fazed him and he never panicked. With someone like that by your side in a crisis you will always come out on top!

There is a very good reason why I've spent a couple of paragraphs telling you about the Royal Marines I've had the pleasure to work with. If you want to become a Commando then you're going to have to work very hard. You don't need to be the finished article when you attend the Potential Royal

Marines Course (PRMC), but you do need to have the right mental attitude and physical fitness. I've designed this guide so that it will give you every chance of success. Keep it by your side whilst you are going through selection and take onboard the tips and advice that are most applicable to your circumstances.

Finally, remember that you are trying to join something extraordinary. Commandos are different from your average person. They have a unique state of mind that allows them to achieve anything. Work on your mindset as much as you do your fitness and your chances of success will increase greatly.

Richard McMunn

CHAPTER I
THE COMMANDO STATE OF MIND

The Commando state of mind is the first thing I'm going to help you to develop. Before I even begin to talk about the selection process, the interview or even the PRMC, you must learn how important it is to adopt the correct state of mind. If you have it, then you are far more likely to succeed and pass the selection process.

Picture the scene, you are at the PRMC and you are taking part in the assault course. You are totally shattered and your body wants to stop. You've simply had enough and you're not sure that your body can take any more. The majority of other candidates have already stopped and you are desperate to give in. What do you do?

The problem with this kind of scenario is that it is new to you. Not many of us find ourselves in these kinds of situations ever in our lifetime. Therefore our minds are not tuned to cope with it, and the natural reaction is to quit. Your muscles are telling your mind that they can't take any more and they

send a signal to your brain basically saying enough's enough! It's at this point that you're going to be different. This is the difference between your average person and a Commando. Regardless of how much you ache, or regardless of how much your body is telling you to quit, your mind will be telling you something completely different. To put it simply, you never give in, even if your body can't move any further along that assault course, you just don't give in.

During my career I've been in this type of situation on numerous occasions. Some of them have been life or death situations. One in particular was whilst serving as a firefighter on White Watch at Maidstone Fire Station. It was approximately 1745 hours on a cold winter's afternoon and I was due to go off shift at 1800 hours. It was a Friday and I was looking forward to going out on the town with my mates. All of a sudden, the bells went down and we were turned out to a fire in a furniture store located in the town centre.

When we arrived, black smoke was billowing out of the front entrance door and windows, and a rather stressful shop owner was urging us to get a move on. As you can imagine, his shop was in serious danger of burning to the ground. I'd not long been out of my recruit training and I had not experienced that many 'severe' fires yet. It was my turn to wear breathing apparatus so I quickly got rigged up, went under air, and then followed the more senior firefighter into the building. What was about to happen was one of the most frightening experiences I have ever encountered in my life. I was about to be tested to the limit.

As we entered the building I could sense something wasn't quite right. The smoke was becoming thicker and blacker by the second and the temperature was rising quickly. The signs of flashover and backdraught were relatively new to

the Fire Service at the time, so we weren't fully aware of the dangerous situation we were entering into. We made our way up to the third floor quickly, taking a hose with us so that we could tackle the fire, and also retrace our steps on the way out. We had been told that the fire was probably in a room on the upper floors of the building, so we started to search for the fire in line with our training and procedures.

After approximately ten minutes the heat inside the building became unbearable, and I couldn't see my hand in front of my face due to the thick, black acrid smoke. I concentrated on my training, took deep breaths and checked my air regularly. I was very fit at the time and hadn't used that much air from my cylinder. My colleague shouted in my ear that he couldn't see the fire anywhere and that maybe we should start thinking about evacuating the building due to the intensity of the heat. I think his words were something more along the lines of "let's get the f#ck out of here, the heat's starting to burn my shoulders!"

Just as we started to retrace our steps we heard a noise that was every firefighter's worst nightmare. Outside, the fire had become so intense that the officer in charge had decided it was time to get us out. Basically, he had initiated the evacuation procedure, which was short blasts of an acme thunderer whistle. All we could hear from inside the building was whistles being blown – we knew we were in trouble. Even though it was a long time ago now, the thought of it still makes the hairs stand up on the back of my neck. I'd heard of incidents where firefighters had lost their lives in fires, and I thought that it might now be my turn.

We quickly started to retrace our steps, following the hose carefully. I'd started to become slightly disorientated due to the heat, but I knew the hose reel would guide us back down

the stairs, and to ultimate safety. How wrong could I be! As we approached the top of the stairs the hose suddenly disappeared. My colleague turned to me and shouted that the hose had become trapped under some fallen furniture and he couldn't find the other end of it – we were now in serious trouble. The hose was basically our lifeline, which would lead us to safety, and now we didn't have it. We sat together and took deep breaths. The whistles were still blaring outside and we knew that the only way to get out of this damn building was to try as hard as possible to conserve our air and remain calm. All I could think about was my girlfriend and how much I wanted to see her again. That thought in my mind gave me the confidence and determination to push on and get out of the building to safety.

We decided to locate a wall, and then simply follow it in the direction that our instincts told us would lead to the top of the stairs. We eventually came to the top of some stairs but there was a problem. We could not locate the hose, which effectively meant that this flight of stairs was not the flight we had used to gain access to the building in the first place. Basically we had no choice, we had to go down them and just hope that they led us outside. As we progressed down the stairs my heart was beating like never before. I remember thinking that these stairs could be leading us to a cellar or basement area and that we would become trapped. Thankfully, as we made our way down the stairs we heard voices. The officer in charge had sent in an emergency crew to help locate us. We met them halfway down the stairs and they then led us out to safety. I can remember making my way outside of the building and looking back at the store, which had already been half demolished by the inferno. Another few minutes in there and I would have been dead, that's for sure. As I took off my breathing apparatus set,

which was caked in soot, the officer in charge looked over at me with a huge sign of relief on his face. If only he knew how I was feeling!

I learnt a tremendous amount from that incident. The first thing I learnt was how important it is to remain calm in every crisis situation. Even when things are really bad, the only way that you'll achieve a successful outcome is by staying calm and focused. The second thing I learnt from that experience was the importance of comradeship and teamwork. The Fire Service is very similar to the Royal Marines in the fact that everyone looks out for each other. Everyone in the team is dependant on each other. You do your job properly and the team will be just fine. Break the rules, be unprofessional or disorganised, and things will go wrong, it's as simple as that!

The Commando state of mind involves the following key areas:

- Confidence
- Strength
- Independence
- Ability

Each one of the above qualities is exceptional in an individual. If you have them all, then you are a serious contender for becoming a Royal Marines Commando. Now I'm not saying that you need to have all of these qualities polished off before you apply to become a Commando, but a knowledge of how important they are and also how to demonstrate them in certain situations will go a long way to helping you succeed. Let's now take a look at each of them individually.

Confidence
Confidence is at the top of the list for me personally when it comes to achieving what I want in life. There is a vast

difference, however, between confidence and arrogance. I am confident because I believe in my own abilities, I work hard to improve on my weak areas, and I also believe in those people around me. I am not afraid to take risks that I believe are worth taking, and I am certainly not afraid to put my own life at risk to save others. Whilst describing earlier the Commandos I've had the pleasure to work with, you will recall that I mentioned how they kept themselves to themselves and quietly got on with their work. They had a confidence about them but they felt no need to show off or brag about who they were or what they were capable of achieving.

Whilst going through selection try to demonstrate confidence, but never cross the line into arrogance. The selection staff want to see that you have the guts to keep running when you're absolutely shattered, and when your body is telling you stop. They want to see that that you have the confidence to put yourself forward, when others around you stand back. Confidence comes with time and with experience, but there is no reason why you can't start improving it right now in preparation for selection.

Strength

To the majority of people, the word 'strength' means the ability to lift heavy weights or objects. To the Commando, it is not just about physical strength, but also about strength of the mind. The only obstacle in your way to passing selection is your own mind. Fill it with doubt and negative thoughts, and the end result is virtually guaranteed to be failure. Yes, of course you must work on your physical strength and fitness, but if your mind isn't tuned into what you want to achieve, then you are going nowhere, fast!

Allow me to give you an example of where strength of mind can work to your advantage. Whilst going through the

selection process for becoming a firefighter, I was required to attend an intense physical assessment day. Amongst other things, the assessment involved a requirement to:

- Bench press 50kg, 20 times within 60 seconds;

- Run around a field for an hour whilst carrying a heavy object between a small group;

- A claustrophobia test involving crawling through sewer pipes in the dark whilst wearing a blacked out mask;

- Assembling items of equipment;

- Knots and lines;

- Hose running.

The hose running assessment was carried out at the end of the day. Out of twenty people who had started the day, there were just six of us left. Although I was exhausted, there was absolutely no way I was going to fail the hose running assessment. This assessment had a reputation for being gruelling. It entailed running out lengths of heavy hose whilst wearing full firefighting uniform, and then making it back up again in a prescribed manner. It sounds like a simple task, but coupled with the sheer exhaustion that was already taking its toll on my body, and the fact that I was wearing ill-fitting firefighter's uniform, this was no easy task.

The Station Officer started off by making us do ten runs, just to warm up. Whilst we were carrying out the runs, a Sub Officer would walk next to us shouting in our ears how 'useless' he thought we were, and that he knew 'how much we wanted to give in.' After the first ten runs we were then required to do a further 25 more in succession. Soon after we started two men dropped out, leaving just the four of us remaining. We all managed to complete the 25 runs

although I was ready crumble and I know for certain that I couldn't have done any more. We all stood there in a line with our hoses made up, ready for the next set of instructions. The Station Officer walked up and down with his stick and clipboard, making us wait in anticipation – he was clearly loving every minute of it! My legs were shaking and I could feel my heart pounding so fast it felt like it was about to jump out of my skin.

Then, the Station Officer spoke once more – "OK, pick up your hoses and get ready for another 25 runs!" 25 more runs I thought! You must be joking!

At that point I was at a crossroads in my life. Give in now and all that hard work training to pass firefighter selection would be out of the window. But if I try to press on, then there's absolutely no way I can manage another 25 runs! It was at that point that a thought came into my mind. Whether I could do the next set of 25 runs or not was irrelevant. What was important was that I carried on and I didn't give in. So I did. I picked up my hose and waited for the Station Officer to tell us to commence. He then turned round and said – "Well done guys, you've passed. Put the hoses down and grab yourselves a glass of water." I couldn't believe it; the b#stard was just testing us to see if we had the strength of mind to continue, even though our bodies couldn't take anymore – a valuable lesson in determination and strength of mind if ever I saw one.

Mindset is extremely important whilst preparing for selection. You will need to be organised and disciplined and you will need to concentrate on improving your weak areas. During a later chapter I will explain how to use an action plan, which is designed to lead you to success. Remember that the quality of strength is not just about lifting or carrying heavy objects, but the strength of your mind also.

Independence

The quality of independence is all about being able to look after yourself and being capable of carrying out your role within the team to a professional standard. Once you've completed the rigorous Royal Marines Commando training course, you will be expected to look after yourself, your kit and your life in general. Yes there will be continuous training exercises and development sessions, but the overall maintenance of your kit, weapons and physical fitness is down to you. Neglect any of these important elements and you will be letting yourself and the team down.

Royal Marines depend on each other. You will depend on your colleagues within the Corp to carry out their job to a high standard, and they will depend on you also.

Ability

Ability is the quality of being able to do something, especially the physical and mental power to accomplish something.

Not everyone has the ability to become a Royal Marines Commando. That's one of the reasons why the Corp have used the strap line '99.9% need not apply' during past recruitment campaigns. It wasn't designed to put people off, but more importantly designed to make people aware that you need a large amount of 'ability', not only to pass the selection process, but also to become a competent Marine. If you have the ability, then you can be trained.

The Commando State of Mind should not only be something that you learn, but it should also be something that you strive to demonstrate during selection. Have the confidence in your own abilities, have the strength of mind to achieve and persevere; be independent and also have the ability to learn new things and accomplish your goals.

TOP TIPS ON HOW TO PREPARE FOR, AND PASS THE ROYAL MARINES SELECTION PROCESS

TIP I
The right mental approach

Without the correct mental approach your chances of passing selection will be limited. The majority of people who fail the Potential Royal Marines Course do so during the first 3-mile run of the first day. Even though they are told that they must pass this, many candidates turn up unprepared. This basically means that they don't have the right mental approach. If they can't be arsed to make sure they are capable of running 1.5 miles in a certain time, then what chance do they have of passing the training course?

It is vital that you approach your preparation for selection in the right frame of mind. This means getting up early every morning and making sure you can easily pass all of the minimum standards expected during selection. It is also about having the mindset that you will not give in, despite what your body will be telling you. There will be times during selection when you've simply had enough. These are the times when you must push yourself forward and keep going despite the fatigue and the physical agony.

TIP 2
Use an action plan to ensure success

Action plans are a great way to measure your progress during pre-selection preparation. I use an action plan in just about everything I do that is work related. An action plan basically sets out what you intend to do, and when you intend to do it. An example of a very basic action plan that is focused on fitness preparation might look like this:

Monday 6am start, run 3 miles (best effort), record my time.

Tuesday 6 am start, 50 press-ups, 50 sit-ups, making sure I concentrate on the correct technique.

Wednesday 10-mile run, then 50 sit-ups and 50 press-ups, making sure I concentrate on the correct technique.

Thursday Swim 25 lengths of my local swimming pool (breaststroke).

Friday 6am start, 10 pull-ups, 50 press-ups and 50 sit-ups, making sure I concentrate on the correct technique.

Saturday Rest day.

Sunday 5-mile brisk walk.

During the next week you may decide to increase the intensity of your workouts and the number of repetitions that you are performing.

The point I am trying to make here is that if you use an action plan, you are far more likely to make significant progress. If you stick the action plan in a prominent position at home, such as the fridge door, then it will act as a reminder of what you need to do the following day.

TIP 3
Don't neglect your aptitude testing ability
Whilst I recommend that you spend the majority of your pre-selection preparation working hard on your fitness, you should not neglect the important area of aptitude testing. During the selection process you will be required to pass an aptitude test, which will consist of a number of tests including numerical reasoning, verbal ability and mechanical comprehension. I recommend that you spend at least 30 minutes every evening of the week working on your ability

to pass these tests. Within this guide I have provided you with lots of sample test questions to assist you during your preparation. You may also decide to obtain additional testing resources through the website www.how2become.co.uk.

TIP 4
Train hard, race easy
If somebody finds a test or assessment easy, it generally means that they have prepared hard for it. If you work hard in the weeks leading up to the PRMC, then you should find that you pass it with very few problems. Yes, you will find it tough, but if you've trained above the minimum standards that are required, then you will pass with flying colours.

When I was 26 I decided to carry out an Iron Man challenge for a local charity. This involved swimming 2 miles, then running a marathon, before finishing off with a 120-mile cycle ride. I managed to achieve all of this within 9 hours. Whilst it was mentally tough, the physical aspect was easy. It was easy because I'd trained extremely hard in the 6 months leading up to the challenge. Train hard in the build up to selection, and you will certainly race easy!

TIP 5
Bleep test preparation
Lots of people neglect to try out the bleep test before they go through selection. During the PRMC you will be required to reach level 13, so make sure you can easily achieve this before you go. There are no excuses for not getting yourself a copy of the test and practising it. You can obtain a copy of the test at www.how2become.co.uk. Alternatively, you can download a copy of the test, and get yourself lots of tips and advice on how to prepare for Royal Marines selection, at the following website: **www.royalmarinestraining.co.uk**

TIP 6
Technique is crucial
During the PRMC you will be required to carry out a number of sit-ups, press-ups and pull-ups, within a two-minute period. Being able to reach the minimum standard is only part of it; you must also perform them using the correct technique. During the build up to selection make sure you practise each of the above utilising the correct technique. I will explain the correct technique during the PRMC section of the guide. This will not only make your life a lot easier during the PRMC, but it will also impress the instructors and show them that you have really gone out of your way to meet their requirements.

TIP 7
You are what you eat (and drink)
Let's face it; a diet of lager, burgers, chips and kebabs isn't going to help you get the most out of your training sessions. In the build up to selection fill yourself with the right types of foods and also make sure you drink plenty of water. You will need the water to keep yourself hydrated.

Foods such as fish, chicken, vegetables, fruit, rice and potatoes are all rich in the right types of nutrients, which will allow you to perform to the best of your ability. Try to cut out caffeine, alcohol and all forms of takeaway food in the build up to selection. You will feel a lot better for it and you will be able to work harder and longer.

TIP 8
Practise a mock interview
Before you attend the AFCO interview, and even the PRMC, try out a mock interview at home. A mock interview basically involves getting a friend or relative to sit down and ask you all of the interview questions that are contained within

this guide. This will give you the opportunity to practise your responses to the questions before you do the real thing. The Royal Marines selecting officers are looking for people who are confident in their own abilities. During the interview you will want to portray a level of confidence and you can achieve this by working through your answers before you attend the real thing.

I also recommend that you work on your interview technique. This involves:

- Walking into the interview room looking smart and well presented. Stand tall and do not slouch.

- Don't sit down in the interview chair until invited to do so.

- Be respectful and courteous towards the interview panel. Address them as 'sir' unless told otherwise.

- Maintain eye contact during the interview, but don't stare them out!

- Never slouch in the interview chair. Sit upright at all times and do not fidget.

- When responding to the interview questions avoid any form of waffle or bullsh#t. They will see right through it. Be honest in your responses at all times.

Now let's move on to the next section of the guide where we will look at the selection process for becoming a Royal Marines Commando.

CHAPTER 2
THE ROYAL MARINES COMMANDO SELECTION PROCESS

The selection process for becoming a Royal Marines Commando consists of the following elements:

Step 1
Contact the Careers Advisors

Step 2
Armed Forces Careers Office visit

Step 3
Aptitude test

Step 4
Interview and medical check

Step 5
Pre-joining fitness test

Step 6
Potential Royal Marines Course (PRMC)

 how2become

STEP 1 – CONTACT THE CAREERS ADVISORS

The first step in your pursuit to joining the Royal Marines is to contact your local Royal Navy careers office. Right from the offset it is important that you create the right impression. When you speak to the recruitment advisor make sure you are polite and courteous. There is nothing wrong with you addressing them as 'Sir' or 'Ma'am', and if you do, you will be creating a positive impression right from the offset. One of the selection criteria at these early stages is your reaction to regimentation, discipline and routine. If you can show that you have respect for regimentation and for people in positions of authority, then you will be scoring higher marks than your average candidate.

When speaking to the recruitment advisor, he or she may ask you a number of initial questions relating to whether or not you have any criminal convictions, or whether you have or have had asthma at any time during your life. It is important that you are honest at every stage of the process. If you are not, they could find out at a later point and this may jeopardise your chances.

Make sure you have a pen and paper with you when you make your initial telephone call. Also remember to have a diary with you as they may invite you to attend for an initial chat at the Careers Office. Make a note of any meeting dates and ask questions if you are unsure about parking or directions etc. Alternatively, they may send an information pack for you to read and digest. When you receive the information pack read it thoroughly. It will contain lots of important information about life within the Royal Marines including a choice of careers. You will find that during the interview you will be asked questions relating to the information contained within the recruitment literature.

STEP 2 – ARMED FORCES CAREERS OFFICE VISIT

Your initial meeting with the Royal Marines Careers Advisor is as important as any other and it is an opportunity for you to create a positive impression. Don't be late for your appointment and be sure to check the route to the Careers Office prior to any scheduled meeting. If you are travelling by car make sure you know where to park, or if you are taking public transport then check train/bus times as these can be unreliable.

It is also worth taking a note of the Careers Office telephone number, just in case your car breaks down or you anticipate being late. They will appreciate a courtesy call if you are going to be late and in the majority of circumstances they will reschedule your meeting if you have to cancel due to unforeseen circumstances.

STEP 3 – APTITUDE TEST

The aptitude test is designed to assess your ability to work effectively with language, numbers, reasoning and mechanical comprehension. Within later sections of this guide I have provided you with lots of sample test questions to help you prepare.

STEP 4 – INTERVIEW AND MEDICAL CHECK

During the selection process you will be interviewed both at the Armed Forces Careers Office (AFCO) and also during the PRMC. They will want to know why you want to become a Royal Marines Commando, what you have done to find out about the service, and how you think you will cope with the training. Once you have passed the interview you will need to undertake a medical check to make sure that you are in good health.

Within a later section of the guide I have provided you with lots of sample interview questions and responses to help you prepare for the interview.

STEP 5 – PRE-JOINING FITNESS TEST (PJFT)

The majority of candidates who fail the Potential Royal Marines Course (PRMC) do so during the 3-mile run. Therefore, the Royal Marines want to be sure that you can pass this prior to sending you off to PRMC. The PJFT consists of two 2.4km runs; the first run to be completed within 12mins 30secs, the second run, to be best effort, but within 10mins 30secs, with a minute rest in between the two runs. The runs are to be conducted on a 2 degree inclination on the running machine.

STEP 6 – THE POTENTIAL ROYAL MARINES COURSE (PRMC)

The Potential Royal Marines Course lasts for 2½ days, during which time you will be assessed in the gym; on the assault course; on a 3-mile run; during an interview and in the classroom. You will also meet some recruits who are going through their training to find out what it is really like.

At the end of day three, they will let you know whether they think you have what it takes to be trained as a Royal Marines Commando. If you pass, then you will receive a joining date.

During a later section of the guide I have provided you with details on how you can effectively prepare for the different elements of the selection process.

CHAPTER 3
THE ROYAL NAVY RECRUITING TEST

As part of the Royal Marines selection process you will be required to pass the Royal Navy Recruiting Test. The test covers the following four areas

- A reasoning test

- A verbal ability test

- A numeracy test

- A mechanical reasoning test

The tests are usually carried out at the Armed Forces Careers Office and will be under strict timed conditions. Details of the time restrictions and number of questions per exercise will be provided in your recruitment literature.

Within this section of the guide I have provided you with a large number of sample test questions relating to each

section to help you prepare. Please note that the questions I have provided are NOT the actual questions that you will be presented with at the test. They are provided as a useful practice tool to help you improve your scores during the real test. Work through each section carefully, sticking to the times that I have provided. At the end of each test go back and check to see which, if any, you got wrong. Learning from your mistakes is a crucial part of the selection process.

6. Rachel runs faster than her sister Georgia.

Who runs the slowest?

Answer

7. David has more money than Arnold.

Who is the poorer?

Answer

8. Jill is weaker than Bill.

Who is the strongest?

Answer

Hayley sleeps for 10 hours and Julie sleeps for 50 minutes.

Who sleeps the longest?

Answer

Sadie's shoe size is 7 and Mary's is 9.

Who needs the larger size shoes?

Answer

CHAPTER 4
THE REASONING TEST

During the Royal Navy Recruiting Test you will be required to sit a Reasoning Test. During the test you will have 9 minutes in which to answer 30 questions.

An example of a reasoning test question is as follows:

Sample Question I

Richard is taller than Steven. Who is shorter?

The answer in this case would be Steven as the statement indicates that Richard is taller than Steven, so therefore Steven is the shorter of the two.

Answer: Steven

Here is another example:

Sample Question 2

Mark is not as wealthy as Jane. Who has less money?

The answer in this case would be Mark. The statement indicates that Mark is not as wealthy as Jane, therefore implying that Jane has more money. Mark therefore has less money and is not as wealthy as Jane. When you are answering this type of question it is important that you READ the question very carefully. The questions are relatively simple but they can catch you out if you do not read them properly.

Answer: Mark

Now take a look at another example:

Sample Question 3

Car is to motorway as aeroplane is to:

   A. Sky

   B. Wing

   C. Holiday

   D. Cabin crew

   E. Sun

The answer is A – Sky. This is because a *car* travels on a *motorway* and an *aeroplane* travels in the *sky*.

Now try the exercise on the following page, which contains 30 sample reasoning test questions. Allow yourself 9 minutes to complete the exercise.

Once you have finished the exercise, take a look at the answers and see how well you performed. If you got any wrong try to understand the reason why so that can improve next time.

REASONING TEST EXERCISE 1

1. Marcus is not as bright as Andrew.

Who is brighter?

Answer

2. Sharon is taller than Sheila

Who is the tallest?

Answer

3. Pauline is stronger than Beverley.

Who is the weaker of the two?

Answer

4. Gary is lighter than Frederick.

Who is the heavier?

Answer

5. The black car is faster than the white

Which car is the quickest?

Answer

9.
65

W

An

10.

Who

Answ

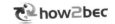

11. George is sadder than Mark.

Who is the happier of the two?

Answer

12. Pete is faster than Rick.

Who is the slowest?

Answer

13. Jim is older than Brian.

Who is the youngest?

Answer

14. Katie eats slower than Lucy.

Who is the faster eater?

Answer

15. John finishes the race before Tony.

Who ran the slowest?

Answer

16. Ink is to pen as water is to?

A. Wash   **B.** Fish   **C.** Lake   **D.** Drink   **E.** Cold

Answer [   ]

17. Car is to drive as aeroplane is to?

A. Holiday   **B.** Cabin Crew   **C.** Airport   **D.** Fly   **E.** Wing

Answer [   ]

18. Tall is to short as thick is to?

A. Long   **B.** Length   **C.** Line   **D.** Thin   **E.** Metre

Answer [   ]

19. Train is to track as ship is to?

A. Harbour   **B.** Sea   **C.** Sail   **D.** Stern   **E.** Hull

Answer [   ]

20. If the following words were arranged in alphabetical order, which one would come second?

A. Believe   **B.** Beast   **C.** Belief   **D.** Bereaved   **E.** Best

Answer [   ]

21. If the following words were arranged in alphabetical order, which one would come last?

A. Desire   **B.** Desired   **C.** Desirable   **D.** Deserted   **E.** Desert

Answer

22. Walk is to run as slow is to?

A. Fast   **B.** Speed   **C.** Quicker   **D.** Pace   **E.** Stop

Answer

23 Sun is to hot as ice is to?

A. Melt   **B.** Winter   **C.** Icicle   **D.** Freeze   **E.** Cold

Answer

24. Hammer is to nail as bat is to?

A. Fly   **B.** Ball   **C.** Cricket   **D.** Cat   **E.** Hit

Answer

25. Book is to read as music is to?

A. Note   **B.** Instrument   **C.** Listen   **D.** Dance   **E.** Piano

Answer

26. Which of the following words contains the most vowels?

A. Reasonable **B.** Combination **C.** Vegetables **D.** Audaciously

Answer

27. Which of the following words contains the least vowels?

A. Barber   **B.** Radio   **C.** Disastrous   **D.** Elephant **E.** March

Answer

28. Chair is to sit as ladder is to?

A. Climb   **B.** Step   **C.** Bridge   **D.** Metal   **E.** Heavy

Answer

29. Mark can run faster than Jane. Jane can run faster than Nigel who is slower than Bill. Bill runs faster than Mark. Who is the slowest?

A. Nigel   **B.** Jane   **C.** Bill   **D.** Mark

Answer

30. If the following words were placed in alphabetical order, which one would come third?

A. Delightful   **B.** Delicious   **C.** Delayed   **D.** Delicate

Answer

Now that you have completed reasoning exercise 1, take the time to work through the answers before moving on to the second reasoning exercise.

ANSWERS TO REASONING TEST EXERCISE 1

1.	Andrew	**16.**	C
2.	Sharon	**17.**	D
3.	Beverley	**18.**	D
4.	Frederick	**19.**	B
5.	The black car	**20.**	C
6.	Georgia	**21.**	B
7.	Arnold	**22.**	A
8.	Bill	**23.**	E
9.	Julie	**24.**	B
10.	Mary	**25.**	C
11.	Mark	**26.**	D
12.	Rick	**27.**	E
13.	Brian	**28.**	A
14.	Lucy	**29.**	A
15.	Tony	**30.**	B

REASONING EXERCISE 2

During the Royal Navy Recruiting Test you will find that the reasoning exercise may contain questions in diagrammatic format. Take a look at the following sample question.

Sample Question I

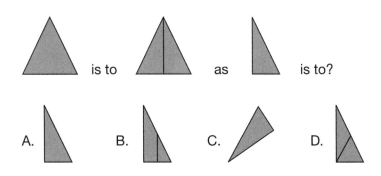

You will notice in the question that the straight line runs vertically through the centre of the triangle. Therefore, the correct answer to the question is B, as the straight line runs vertically through the shape.

Take a look at the next question.

Sample Question 2

Which of the following comes next?

A.   B.   C.   D.

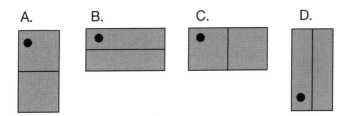

The correct answer is C. You will notice in the sample question that the black dot is moving around the shapes in a clockwise manner. It starts off in the top right hand corner of the first shape. Then it progresses to the bottom right hand corner of the second shape before moving round to the bottom left hand corner of the third shape. Similarly, the first shape has a horizontal line through it, the second has a vertical line through it, the third a horizontal line again, and so the fourth shape should have a vertical line through it. Therefore C, where the black dot is in the top left hand corner of the shape and a vertical line divides the shape, is the correct answer.

Now try Reasoning Test Exercise 2, which contains sample diagrammatic test questions. You have 9 minutes in which to answer 30 questions.

REASONING TEST EXERCISE 2

Question I

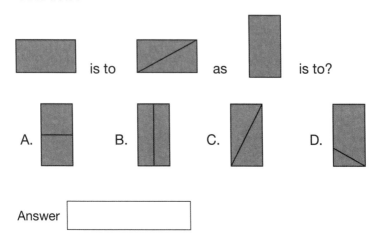

Answer [   ]

Question 2

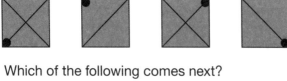

Which of the following comes next?

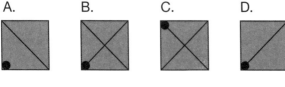

Answer [   ]

Question 3

Which of the following comes next?

A.   B.   C.   D.

Answer [   ]

Question 4

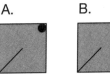 is to as is to?

A.   B. C.   D.

Answer [   ]

Question 5

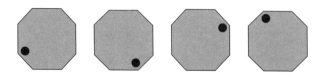

Which of the following comes next?

A.   B.   C.   D.

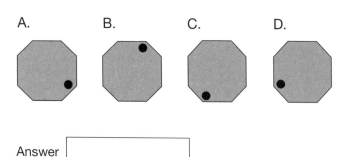

Answer [   ]

Question 6

Which of the following comes next?

A.   B.   C.   D.

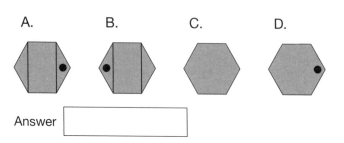

Answer [   ]

Question 7

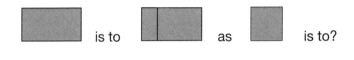

A. B. C. D.

Answer

Question 8

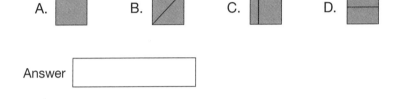

Which of the following comes next?

A.   B.   C.   D.

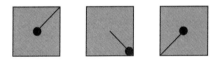

Answer

Question 9

Which of the following comes next?

A.   B.   C.   D.

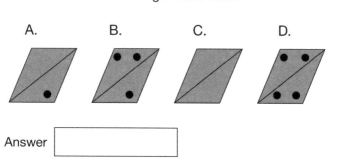

Answer [   ]

Question 10

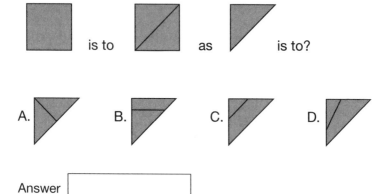

is to   as   is to?

A.   B.   C.   D.

Answer [   ]

Question II

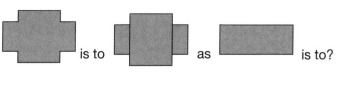

A.   B.   C.   D.

Answer [   ]

Question I2

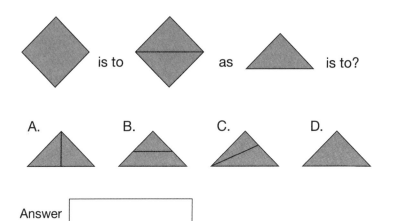

A.   B.   C.   D.

Answer [   ]

Question 13

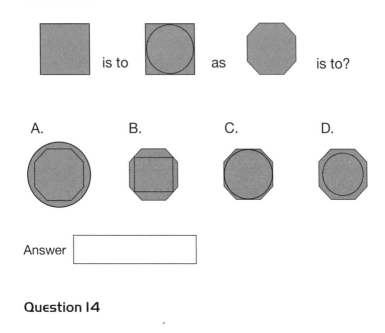

Answer [   ]

Question 14

Answer [   ]

Question 15

Which of the following comes next?

A.   B.   C.   D.

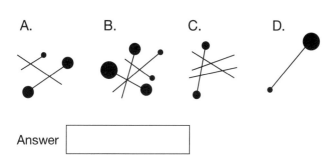

Answer

Question 16

A.   B.   C.   D.

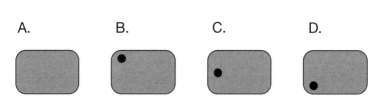

Answer

Question 17

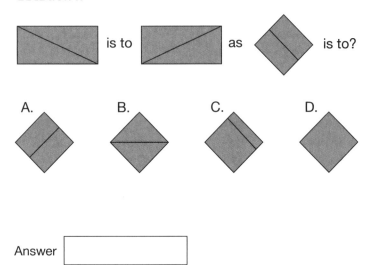

Answer [   ]

Question 18

Which of the following comes next?

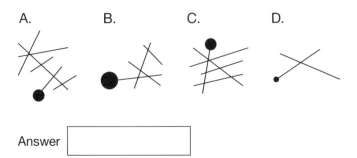

Answer [   ]

Question 19

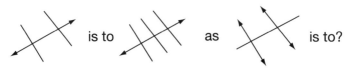

A.   B.   C.   D.

Answer [   ]

Question 20

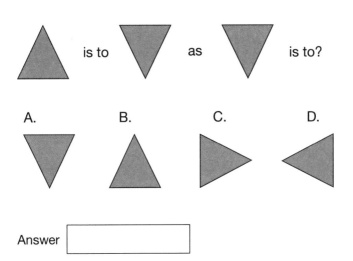

Answer [   ]

how2become

Question 21

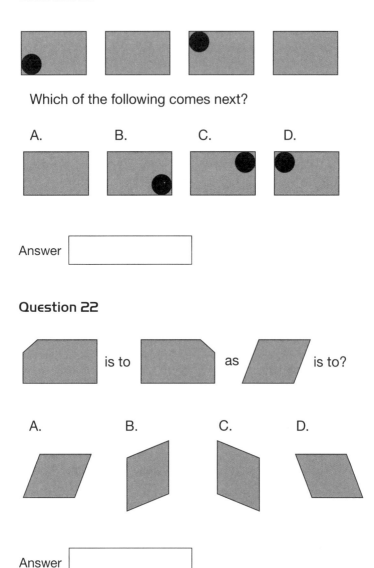

Which of the following comes next?

A.   B.   C.   D.

Answer [   ]

Question 22

is to   as   is to?

A.   B.   C.   D.

Answer [   ]

Question 23

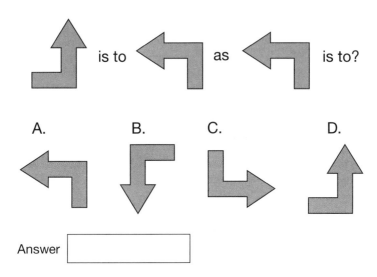

A.   B.   C.   D.

Answer [   ]

Question 24

Which of the following comes next?

A.   B.   C.   D.

Answer [   ]

Question 25

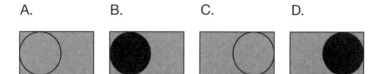

Answer

Question 26

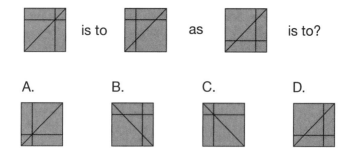

Answer

Question 27

Which of the following comes next?

A. 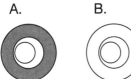 B. C. D.

Answer

Question 28

 is to as is to?

A. B. C. D.

Answer

Question 29

Which of the following comes next?

A. B. C. D.

Answer

Question 30

Which of the following comes next?

A. B. C. D.

Answer

Now that you have completed reasoning test exercise 2 take the time to work through the answers, carefully checking to see which, if any, you got wrong.

ANSWERS TO REASONING TEST EXERCISE 2

1.	C	**16.**	C
2.	B	**17.**	A
3.	B	**18.**	A
4.	A	**19.**	C
5.	D	**20.**	B
6.	C	**21.**	C
7.	C	**22.**	D
8.	A	**23.**	B
9.	D	**24.**	C
10.	C	**25.**	C
11.	A	**26.**	A
12.	B	**27.**	A
13.	C	**28.**	D
14.	A	**29.**	B
15.	B	**30.**	A

REASONING TEST EXERCISE 3

During the Royal Navy Recruiting Test you will find that the reasoning exercise may contain questions in numerical format. Take a look at the following sample question.

Sample Question I

Take a look at the following row of numbers. Which number comes next from the options available?

16, 18, 20, 22, 24, 26, ?

A. 28   B. 30   C. 32   D. 34   E. 36

The answer is A. 28. The numbers are rising by 2 each time.

Now take a look at the next sample question.

Sample Question 2

Take a look at the following row of numbers. Which number represents '?' from the options available?

8, 2, 10, 4, 12, 16, ?, 256

A. 8   B. 14   C. 16   D. 20   E. 24

The answer is B. 14. The 1st, 3rd and 5th odd numbers in the row are increasing by 2 each time, which means the 7th number in the row will be 14. You will also notice that the 2nd, 4th and 6th even numbers are being multiplied by themselves in order to reach the next even number, e.g. 2 x 2 = 4, 4 x 4 = 16, 16 x 16 = 256.

Once you understand what is required in the test, move on to the following exercise. There are 30 questions and you have a total of 9 minutes in which to answer them.

REASONING TEST EXERCISE 3

Question I

Take a look at the following row of numbers. Which number represents '?' from the options available?

1, 3, 5, ?, 9, 11, 13

A. 6   B. 7   C. 8   D. 9   E. 10

Answer

Question 2

Take a look at the following row of numbers. Which number represents '?' from the options available?

11, 12, 14, 17, 21, ?, 32

A. 22   B. 23   C. 24   D. 25   E. 26

Answer

Question 3

Take a look at the following row of numbers. Which number represents '?' from the options available?

10, 25, 40, ?, 70, 85, 100

A. 35   B. 40   C. 45   D. 50   E. 55

Answer

Question 4

Take a look at the following row of numbers. Which number comes next from the options available?

5, 10, 10, 20, 15, 30, ?

A. 20   B. 25   C. 30   D. 35   E. 40

Answer

Question 5

Take a look at the following row of numbers. Which number comes next from the options available?

100, 12, 80, 14, 60, 16, ?

A. 18   B. 20   C. 80   D. 40   E. 22

Answer

Question 6

Take a look at the following row of numbers. Which number comes next from the options available?

50, 2, 57, 4, 64, ?, 71

A. 70   B. 78   C. 16   D. 85   E. 256

Answer

Question 7

Take a look at the following row of numbers. Which number comes next from the options available?

3, 15, 9, 30, 15, 45, 21, 60, ?

A. 27   B. 28   C. 75   D. 42   E. 29

Answer

Question 8

Take a look at the following row of numbers. Which number represents '?' from the options available?

2, 4, 9, 11, 16, ?, 23

A. 17   B. 18   C. 19   D. 20   E. 21

Answer

Question 9

Take a look at the following row of numbers. Which number comes next from the options available?

1, 25, 4, 22, 7, 19, 10, 16, 13, ?

A. 16   B. 15   C. 14   D. 13   E. 12

Answer

Question 10

Take a look at the following row of numbers. Which number comes next from the options available?

5, 10, 8, 13, 14, 19, 26, 31, ?

A. 24   B. 32   C. 52   D. 62   E. 50

Answer

Question 11

Take a look at the following row of numbers. Which number comes next from the options available?

5, 10, 4, 11, 3, 12, ?

A. 1   B. 13   C. 2   D. 14   E. 3

Answer

Question 12

Take a look at the following row of numbers. Which number comes next from the options available?

90, 80, 71, 63, 56, 50, ?

A. 45   B. 44   C. 43   D. 42   E. 241

Answer

Question 13

Take a look at the following row of numbers. Which number represents '?' from the options available?

?, 20, 22, 25, 29, 34, 40

A. 15   B. 16   C. 17   D. 18   E. 19

Answer

Question 14

Take a look at the following row of numbers. Which number represents '?' from the options available?

?, 6, 12, 18, 24, 30, 36

A. 2   B. 4   C. 5   D. 0   E. 1

Answer

Question 15

Take a look at the following row of numbers. Which two numbers in order of sequence represent '?' from the options available?

0, 1, 15, 8, 30, 15, 45, 22, ?, ?

A. 50 + 29   B. 50 + 19   C. 15 + 29   D. 60 + 29   E. 55 + 29

Answer

Question 16

Take a look at the following row of numbers. Which two numbers in order of sequence represent '?' from the options available?

?, 11, 4, 22, 8, 33, 16, ?,

A. 2 + 44   B. 0 + 44   C. 2 + 32   D. 2 + 55   E. = + 55

Answer [   ]

Question 17

Take a look at the following row of numbers. Which two numbers in order of sequence represent '?' from the options available?

3, 20, 6, 17, 12, 11, 21, ?, ?

A. 4 + 33   B. 2 + 33   C. 3 + 31   D. 1 + 31   E. 1 + 33

Answer [   ]

Question 18

Take a look at the following row of numbers. Which number comes next from the options available?

16, 20, 25, 31, 38, 46, ?

A. 52   B. 53   C. 55   D. 54   E. 56

Answer [   ]

Question 19

Take a look at the following row of numbers. Which number comes next from the options available?

3, 9, 27, 81, ?

A. 239   B. 240   C. 241   D. 242   E. 243

Answer

Question 20

Take a look at the following row of numbers. Which number comes next from the options available?

33, 35, 39, 45, 53, 63, ?

A. 75   B. 76   C. 77   D. 78   E. 79

Answer

Question 21

Take a look at the following row of numbers. Which number comes next from the options available?

98, 6, 92, 12, 86, 18, 80, ?

A. 76   B. 74   C. 70   D. 12   E. 24

Answer

Question 22

Take a look at the following row of numbers. Which number comes next from the options available?

44, 40, 40, 36, 36, 32, 32, ?

A. 22   B. 28   C. 30   D. 26   E. 24

Answer [   ]

Question 23

Take a look at the following row of numbers. Which three numbers in order of sequence represent '?' from the options available?

2, 22, ?, 20, 6, ?, 8, 16, 10, 14, ?

A. 21 + 18 + 12
B. 4 + 12 + 16
C. 4 + 18 + 12
D. 2 + 18 + 12
E. 2 + 16 + 12

Answer [   ]

Question 24

Take a look at the following row of numbers. Which number comes next from the options available?

85, 7, 80, 15, 70, 23, 55, 31, ?

A. 30   B. 35   C. 40   D. 45   E. 50

Answer [   ]

Question 25

Take a look at the following row of numbers. Which number comes next from the options available?

701, 202, 601, 402, 501, 602, 401, ?

A. 308   B. 301   C. 208   D. 802   E. 206

Answer

Question 26

Take a look at the following row of numbers. Which three numbers in order of sequence represent '?' from the options available?

?, ?, 6, 4, 9, 6, 12, 8, 15, ?

A. 3 + 6 + 10
B. 0 + 2 + 10
C. 3 + 2 + 10
D. 3 + 3 + 10
E. 3 + 2 + 18

Answer

Question 27

Take a look at the following row of numbers. Which number comes next from the options available?

99, 90, 91, 82, 84, 75, 78, 69, ?

A.75   B. 71   C. 76   D. 70   E. 73

Answer

Question 28

Take a look at the following row of numbers. Which two numbers in order of sequence represent '?' from the options available?

?, 22, 35, 18, 39, 14, 43, 10, 47, 6, ?

A. 31 + 51   B. 31 + 44   C. 20 + 51   D. 16 + 51   E. 31 + 49

Answer [   ]

Question 29

Take a look at the following row of numbers. Which number comes next from the options available?

6, 12, 24, 48, 96, 192, 384, ?

A. 786   B. 768   C. 867   D. 764   E. 784

Answer [   ]

Question 30

Take a look at the following row of numbers. Which number comes next from the options available?

6, 9, 13, 18, 24, 31, ?

A. 35   B. 30   C. 40   D. 39   E. 49

Answer [   ]

Now that you've completed exercise 3, work through your answers carefully checking to see which, if any, you got wrong.

ANSWERS TO REASONING TEST EXERCISE 3

1. B
2. E
3. E
4. A
5. D
6. C
7. A
8. B
9. D
10. E
11. C
12. A
13. E
14. D
15. D

16. A
17. B
18. C
19. E
20. A
21. E
22. B
23. C
24. B
25. D
26. C
27. E
28. A
29. B
30. D

CHAPTER 5
THE VERBAL ABILITY TEST

During this part of the test you will be required to answer 30 questions in 9 minutes, which equates to an average of approximately 18 seconds per question. This test is designed to assess your English language skills. The test is multiple choice in nature and in the real test you will have 5 options to choose from. The most effective way to prepare for this type of test is to practise sample questions under timed conditions. Other ways for improving your ability include carrying out crosswords, wordsearches or any other tests that require an ability to work with the English language. You may also decide to purchase your own psychometric test booklet, which can be obtained from all good websites including www.how2become.co.uk.

Take a look at the following sample question.

Sample Question I

Which of the following words is the odd one out?

A. Spanner   B. Pliers   C. Hammer   D. Brush   E. Drill

The answer is D – Brush. This is because all of the other items are tools and the brush is an item used for cleaning, therefore the odd one out.

Now take a look at the next sample question.

Sample Question 2

The following sentence has one word missing. Which word makes the best sense of the sentence?

He had been _____ for hours and was starting to lose his concentration.

A. studying
B. sleeping
C. complaining
D. walk
E. targeting

The correct answer is A – studying, as this word makes best sense of the sentence.

Now try verbal ability test exercise 1. There are 30 questions and you have 9 minutes in which to complete them.

VERBAL ABILITY TEST EXERCISE 1

Question 1

Which of the following words is the odd one out?

A. Car   B. Aeroplane   C. Train   D. Bicycle   E. House

Answer [   ]

Question 2

Which of the following is the odd one out?

A. Right   B. White   C. Dart   D. Bright   E. Sight

Answer [   ]

Question 3

The following sentence has one word missing. Which word makes the best sense of the sentence?

The mechanic worked on the car for 3 hours. At the end of the 3 hours he was…

A. Home   B. Rich   C. Crying   D. Exhausted   E. Thinking

Answer [   ]

Question 4

The following sentence has 2 words missing. Which two words make best sense of the sentence?

The man_____to walk along the beach with his dog. He threw the stick and the dog_____it.

A. hated/chose
B. decided/wanted
C. liked/chased
D. hurried/chased
E. hated/loved

Answer [   ]

Question 5

In the line below, the word outside the brackets will only go with three of the words inside the brackets to make longer words. Which ONE word will it NOT go with?

	A	B	C	D
In	(direct	famous	desirable	cart)

Answer [   ]

Question 6

In the line below, the word outside the brackets will only go with three of the words inside the brackets to make longer words. Which ONE word will it NOT go with?

	A	B	C	D
In	(decisive	reference	destructible	convenience)

Answer [   ]

Question 7

In the line below, the word outside the brackets will only go with three of the words inside the brackets to make longer words. Which ONE word will it NOT go with?

	A	B	C	D
A	(float	bout	part	peck)

Answer

Question 8

Which of the following words is the odd one out?

A. Pink   B. White   C. Red   D. Ball   E. Grey

Answer

Question 9

Which of the following words is the odd one out?

A. Run   B. Jog   C. Walk   D. Sit   E. Sprint

Answer

Question 10

Which of the following words is the odd one out?

A. Eagle   B. Plane   C. Squirrel   D. Cloud   E. Bird

Answer

Question II

Which of the following words is the odd one out?

A. Gold   B. Ivory   C. Platinum   D. Bronze   E. Silver

Answer [   ]

Question 12

Which of the following is the odd one out?

A. Pond   B. River   C. Stream   D. Brook   E. Ocean

Answer [   ]

Question 13

Which of the following is the odd one out?

A. Wood   B. Chair   C. Table   D. Cupboard   E. Stool

Answer [   ]

Question 14

Which three-letter word can be placed in front of the following words to make a new word?

Time   Break   Light   Dreamer

Answer [   ]

Question 15

Which four-letter word can be placed in front of the following words to make a new word?

Box   Bag   Age   Card

Answer

Question 16

The following sentence has one word missing. Which ONE word makes the best sense of the sentence?

After walking for an hour in search of the pub, David decided it was time to turn_____and go back home.

A. up   B. in   C. home   D. around   E. through

Answer

Question 17

The following sentence has one word missing. Which ONE word makes the best sense of the sentence?

We are continually updating the site and would be_____to hear any comments you may have.

A. Pleased   B. Worried   C. Available   D. Suited   E. Scared

Answer

Question 18

The following sentence has two words missing. Which TWO words make the best sense of the sentence?

The Fleet Air Arm is the Royal Navy's air force. It numbers some 6,200 people,_____ is 11.5% of the_____ Royal Naval strength.

A. which/total
B. and/total
C. which/predicted
D. and/corporate
E. which/approximately

Answer

Question 19

The following sentence has one word missing. Which ONE word makes the best sense of the sentence?

The Navy has had to_____ and progress to be ever prepared to defend the British waters from rival forces.

A. develop   B. manoeuvre   C. change   D. seek   E. watch

Answer

Question 20

Which of the following is the odd one out?

A. Cat   B. Dog   C. Hamster   D. Owl   E. Rabbit

Answer

Question 21

Which word best fits the following sentence?

My doctor says I_____ smoke. It's bad for my health.

A. will   B. wouldn't   C. shouldn't   D. like   E. might

Answer

Question 22

Which word best fits the following sentence?

The best thing for a hangover is to go to bed and sleep it

A. through   B. over   C. away   D. in   E. off

Answer

Question 23

Complete the following sentence:

By the time Jane arrived at the disco, Andrew…

A. hadn't gone
B. already left
C. has already Left
D. had stayed
E. had already left

Answer

Question 24

Which of the following words is the odd one out?

A. Lawnmower   B. Hose   C. Rake   D. Carpet   E. Shovel

Answer

Question 25

Complete the following sentence:

Karla was offered the job_____ having poor qualifications.

A. although   B. even though   C. with   D. without   E. despite

Answer

Question 26

Complete the following sentence:

Not only_____ to Glasgow but he also visited many other places in Scotland too.

A. did she
B. did he
C. did he go
D. she went
E. she saw

Answer

Question 27

Complete the following sentence:

Now please remember, you_____ the test until the teacher tells you to.

A. shouldn't
B. will not be starting
C. are not to
D. can't
E. are not to start

Answer

Question 28

Which of the following is the odd one out?

A. Strawberry
B. Raspberry
C. Peach
D. Blackberry
E. Blueberry

Answer

Question 29

Which of the following is the odd one out?

A. Football   B. Wrestling   C. Table tennis   D. Golf   E. Rugby

Answer

Question 30

Which of the following is the odd one out?

A. Man
B. Milkman
C. Secretary
D. Police Officer
E. Firefighter

Answer [   ]

Now that you have completed verbal ability test exercise 1, check your answers carefully before moving on to exercise 2.

ANSWERS TO VERBAL ABILITY TEST EXERCISE 1

1.	E	**16.**	D
2.	C	**17.**	A
3.	D	**18.**	A
4.	C	**19.**	A
5.	D	**20.**	D
6.	B	**21.**	C
7.	D	**22.**	E
8.	D	**23.**	E
9.	D	**24.**	D
10.	C	**25.**	E
11.	B	**26.**	C
12.	A	**27.**	E
13.	A	**28.**	C
14.	Day	**29.**	B
15.	Post	**30.**	A

VERBAL ABILITY TEST EXERCISE 2

Question 1

Which one of the following words relates to the other four?

A. Barbeque
B. Stove
C. Sausages
D. Burger
E. Cooking

Answer [   ]

Question 2

Which one of the following words relates to the other four?

A. Television
B. Acting
C. Entertainment
D. Gig
E. Theatre

Answer [   ]

Question 3

Which one of the following words relates to the other four?

A. Running
B. Fitness
C. Swimming
D. Cycling
E. Rowing

Answer [   ]

Question 4

Which one word inside the brackets will not go with the word outside of the bracket?

Ant   (acid   agonise   eater   implode   hem)

Answer [   ]

Question 5

Which one word inside the brackets will not go with the word outside of the bracket?

Tin   (stone   well   man   smith   foil)

Answer [   ]

Question 6

Which one word inside the brackets will not go with the word outside of the bracket?

Band   (mess   width   wagon   leader   master)

Answer [   ]

Question 7

Which one word inside the brackets will not go with the word outside of the bracket?

Grip   (ping   pier   sack   man   wool)

Answer [   ]

Question 8

Which one word inside the brackets will not go with the word outside of the bracket?

Day   (dream   light   time   room   ball)

Answer [   ]

Question 9

Which of the following sentences has a different meaning to the other four?

A. Richard ended up buying the car for £900.

B. The car was bought by Richard for £900.

C. £900 was the amount Richard spent on the car.

D. The car cost Richard £900.

E. Richard sold the car for £900.

Answer [   ]

Question 10

Which of the following sentences has a different meaning to the other four?

A. Sally spent £350 during her shopping trip.

B. During a shopping trip Sally spent £350.

C. Sally made £350 from her shopping trip.

D. The shopping trip cost Sally £350.

E. A total of £350 was spent during Sally's shopping trip.

Answer [   ]

Question 11

Which of the following sentences has a different meaning to the other four?

A. Barry lost two stone in weight over a period of 4 months.

B. Over a 4 month period Barry gained two stone in weight.

C. Barry put on two stone in 4 months.

D. Over a period of 4 months Barry put on two stone in weight.

E. Two stone was gained in weight by Barry over a 4 month period.

Answer [   ]

Question 12

Which one of the following words relates to the other four?

A. Cardigan

B. Clothes

C. Trousers

D. Shirt

E. Underwear

Answer [   ]

Question 13

Which one of the following words relates to the other four?

A. Pear
B. Apple
C. Banana
D. Pineapple
E. Fruit

Answer

Question 14

Which one of the following words relates to the other four?

A. Communicate
B. E mail
C. Telephone
D. Speak
E. Letter

Answer

Question 15

Which one of the following words relates to the other four?

A. Run
B. Cycle
C. Walk
D. Movement
E. Drive

Answer

Question 16

Which of the following sentences has a different meaning to the other four?

A. The bouncer pushed the man to the floor.

B. The man was pushed to the floor by the bouncer.

C. The bouncer was pushed by the man and he fell to the floor.

D. The bouncer pushed the man and he fell to the floor.

E. The man was pushed by the bouncer to the floor.

Answer

Question 17

Which one word inside the brackets will not go with the word outside of the bracket?

Run   (around   back   charm   lets   off)

Answer

Question 18

Which one word inside the brackets will not go with the word outside of the bracket?

Pot   (hole   stir   belly   ability   able)

Answer

Question 19

Which of the following is the odd one out?

A. Apples
B. Parsnips
C. Peas
D. Sprouts
E. Carrots

Answer [   ]

Question 20

Which of the following is the odd one out?

A. Circle
B. Rectangle
C. Flat
D. Square
E. Sphere

Answer [   ]

Question 21

The following sentence has one word missing. Which word makes the best sense of the sentence?

Sid_____ that he wanted to go home earlier than he originally anticipated.

A. told
B. thought
C. boasted
D. decided
E. suddenly

Answer

Question 22

The following sentence has one word missing. Which word makes the best sense of the sentence?

Tony was often seen walking in the park with _____ dog.

A. one
B. slow
C. his
D. ours
E. them

Answer

Question 23

The following sentence has two words missing. Which two words make the best sense of the sentence?

The album _____ at number one in countries such as the United Kingdom and Canada, and _____ the charts in the United States.

A. peaked / topped
B. reached / topped
C. got / then
D. reached / stormed
E. topped / stormed.

Answer

Question 24

The following sentence has two words missing. Which two word makes the best sense of the sentence?

After four hours of looking, the _____ for the _____ puppy was called off.

A. party / search
B. search / missing
C. dog / missing
D. crying / lovely
E. puppy / lovely.

Answer [   ]

Question 25

Which of the following sentences has a different meaning to the other four?

A. He drove 80 miles to see his fiancée.

B. The man drove 80 miles so that he could see his fiancée.

C. In order to see his fiancée the man drove 80 miles.

D. After driving 80 miles the man was at last with his fiancée.

E. His fiancée had driven 80 miles to see him.

Answer [   ]

Question 26

Which of the following sentences has a different meaning to the other four?

A. It took the man five hours to complete the marathon

B. The man completed the marathon in five hours.

C. The marathon was completed by the man in five hours.

D. Five hours later the man had completed the marathon.

E. The woman would run the marathon in five hours.

Answer [   ]

Question 27

Which one word inside the brackets will not go with the word outside of the bracket?

Run   (away   day   down   over   out)

Answer [   ]

Question 28

Which one word inside the brackets will not go with the word outside of the bracket?

Can   (run   teen   did   non   descent)

Answer [   ]

Question 29

The following sentence has two words missing. Which two words make the best sense of the sentence?

The boy accidentally _____ his ball _____ next doors garden.

A. accidentally / into
B. accidentally / through
C. kicked / into
D. aimed / top
E. kicked / accidentally.

Answer

Question 30

The following sentence has two words missing. Which two words make the best sense of the sentence?

It didn't _____ the man long before he was _____ about the food at the restaurant again.

A. take / complaining
B. need / asking
C. take / complimenting
D. take / eating
E. need / complaining.

Answer

Now that you have completed verbal ability test exercise 2, take the time to work through your answers carefully before moving onto the next test.

ANSWERS TO VERBAL ABILITY TEST EXERCISE 2

1. E

2. C

3. B

4. Implode

5. Well

6. Mess

7. Wool

8. Bal

9. E

10. C

11. A

12. B

13. E

14. A

15. D

16. C

17. Charm

18. Stir

19. A

20. E

21. D

22. C

23. A

24. B

25. E

26. E

27. Day

28. Run

29. C

30. A

CHAPTER 6
THE MECHANICAL COMPREHENSION TEST

During the Royal Navy Recruiting Test you will be required to sit a mechanical comprehension test that consists of 30 questions. You will have just 10 minutes in which to complete the test. Mechanical comprehension tests are an assessment that measures an individual's aptitude to learn mechanical skills. The tests are usually multiple choice in nature and present simple, frequently encountered mechanisms and situations. The majority of mechanical comprehension tests require a working knowledge of basic mechanical operations and the application of physical laws. On the following pages I have provided you with a number of example questions to help you prepare for the tests. Work through them as quickly as possible but remember to go back and check the questions you get wrong; more importantly, make sure you understand how the correct answer is reached.

In this particular exercise there are 20 questions and you have 10 minutes in which to answer them.

MECHANICAL COMPREHENSION TEST 1

Question I

If Circle 'B' turns in a Clockwise direction, which way will circle 'A' turn?

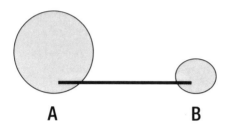

A. Clockwise

B. Anti-Clockwise

C. Backwards and forwards

D. It won't move

Answer

Question 2

Which square is carrying the heaviest load?

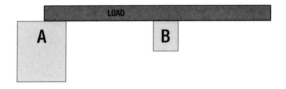

A. Square A

B. Square B

Answer

Question 3

Which pendulum will swing at the slowest speed?

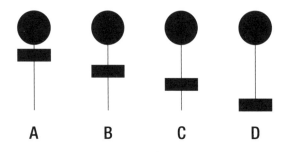

Answer [   ]

Question 4

If Cog 'A' turns in an anti-clockwise direction which way will Cog 'B' turn?

A. Clockwise

B. Anti-Clockwise

Answer [   ]

Question 5

If Cog 'B' moves in a clockwise direction, which way will Cog 'A' turn?

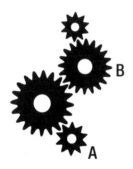

A. Clockwise

B. Anti-Clockwise

Answer ☐

Question 6

Which shelf can carry the greatest load?

 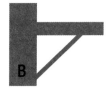

   A. Shelf A

   B. Shelf B

Answer

Question 7

At which point will the pendulum be travelling at the greatest speed?

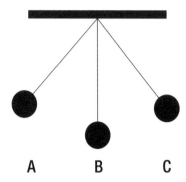

A. Point A

B. Point B

C. Point C

Answer

Question 8

At which point will the beam balance?

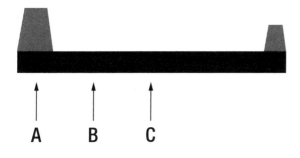

A. Point A

B. Point B

C. Point C

Answer [   ]

Question 9

If water is poured into the narrow tube, up to point 'X', what height would it reach in the wide tube?

A. Point A

B. Point B

C. Point C

Answer

Question 10

At which point would Ball 'Y' have to be at to balance out Ball 'X'?

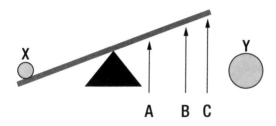

A. Point A

B. Point B

C. Point C

Answer [   ]

Question 11

If Cog 'A' turns anticlockwise, which way will Cog 'F' turn?

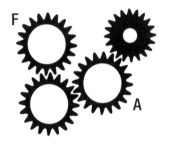

A. Cannot say

B. Clockwise

C. Anti-Clockwise

Answer [   ]

Question 12

Which post is carrying the heaviest load?

A. Both the Same

B. Post X

C. Post Y

Answer

Question 13

If water is poured in at Point D, which tube will overflow first?

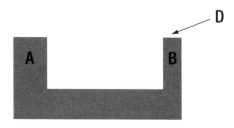

A. Tube A

B. Both the same

C. Tube B

Answer ☐

Question 14

At which point would it be easier to haul up load X?

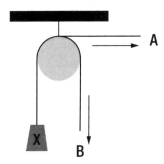

A. Both the Same

B. Point A

C. Point B

Answer [   ]

Question 15

If rope 'A' is pulled in the direction of the arrow, which way will wheel 'C' turn?

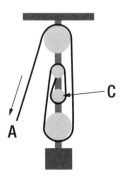

A. Clockwise

B. Anti-clockwise

C. It will not turn

Answer

Question 16

Which load is the heaviest?

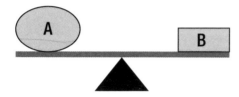

A. Both the Same

B. Load B

C. Load A

Answer [   ]

Question 17

If rope 'A' is pulled in the direction of the arrow, which direction will Load 'Q' travel in?

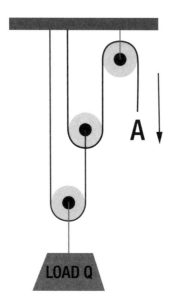

A. It will not move

B. Down

C. Up

Answer [   ]

Question 18

If circle 'X' turns anticlockwise, which way will circle 'Y' turn?

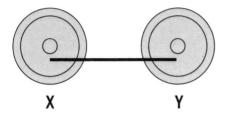

X   Y

  A. Anti-clockwise

  B. Clockwise

  C. Backwards and forwards

Answer

Question 19

Which pulley system will be the easiest to lift the bucket of water?

A. Both the Same

B. Pulley A

C. Pulley B

Answer [   ]

Question 20

At which point(s) will the pendulum be swinging the fastest?

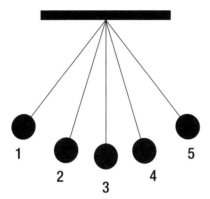

A. Point 1

B. Points 1 and 5

C. Points 3 and 5

D. Point 3

Answer

Now that you have completed mechanical comprehension exercise 1, check your answers carefully before moving onto the exercise 2.

ANSWERS TO MECHANICAL COMPREHENSION TEST 1

1. C

2. B

3. D

4. B

5. A

6. B

7. B

8. B

9. B

10. A

11. C

12. C

13. B

14. C

15. B

16. A

17. C

18. A

19. C

20. D

MECHANICAL COMPREHENSION TEST 2

During mechanical comprehension test 2 you have 10 minutes in which to answer the 20 questions.

Question I

In the following cog and belt system, which cog will rotate the most number of times in an hour?

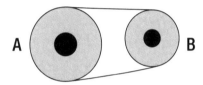

A. Cog A

B. Cog B

C. Both the same

Answer

Question 2

In the following cog and belt system, which cog will rotate the most number of times in thirty minutes?

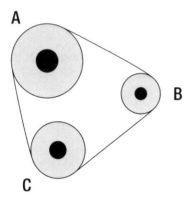

A. Cog A

B. Cog B

C. Both the same

Answer [   ]

Question 3

Which rope would be the easiest to pull the mast over with?

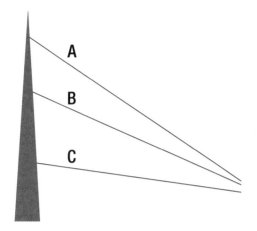

A. Rope A

B. Rope B

C. Rope C

Answer

Question 4

If cog A turns anticlockwise as indicated, which way will cog C turn?

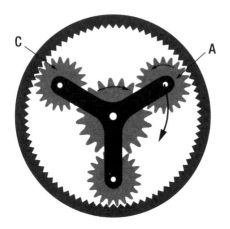

A. Clockwise

B. Anticlockwise

C. Backwards and forwards

Answer

Question 5

If cog A turns clockwise, which way will cog D turn?

A. Clockwise

B. Anticlockwise

C. Backwards and forwards

Answer

Question 6

If wheel D moves anticlockwise at a speed of 100 rpm, how will wheel B move and at what speed?

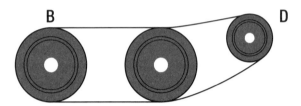

A. Clockwise faster

B. Clockwise slower

C. Anticlockwise faster

D. Anticlockwise slower

Answer

Question 7

Which is the best tool to use for tightening bolts?

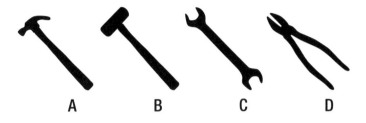

A   B   C   D

Answer [   ]

Question 8

In the following circuit, if switch A closes and switch B remains open, what will happen?

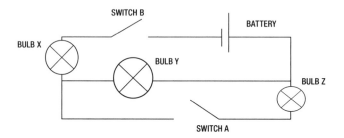

A. Bulbs X, Y, and Z will illuminate.

B. Bulb X will illuminate only.

C. Bulbs Y and Z will illuminate only.

D. No bulbs will illuminate.

Answer [   ]

Question 9

In the following circuit, if switch A closes, what will happen?

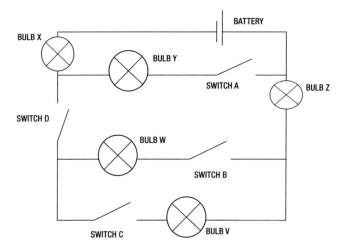

A. Bulbs V, W, X, Y, and Z will illuminate.

B. Bulb X and Y will illuminate only.

C. Bulbs X, Y and Z will illuminate only.

D. No bulbs will illuminate.

Answer

Question 10

The following four containers are filled with clean water to the same level, which is 2 metres in height. If you measured the pressure at the bottom of each container once filled with water, which container would register the highest reading? If you think the reading would be the same for each container then your answer should be E.

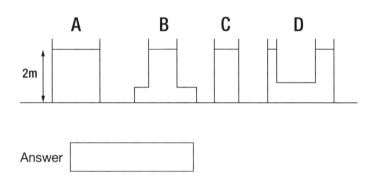

Answer [   ]

Question 11

Which of the following objects is the most unstable? If you think they're all the same then choose F for your answer.

A   B   C   D   E

Answer [   ]

Question 12

How much weight will need to be placed at point X in order to balance out the beam?

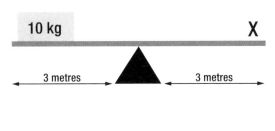

A. 10 kg

B. 15 kg

C. 20 kg

D. 30 kg

E. 100 kg

Answer [   ]

Question 13

Which post is carrying the greatest load?

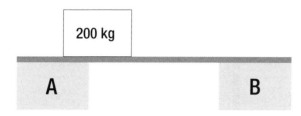

A. Post A

B. Post B

C. Both the same

Answer

Question 14

On the following weighing scales, which is the heaviest load?

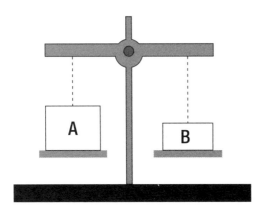

A. Load A

B. Load B

C. Both the same

Answer [   ]

Question 15

At which point should pressurised air enter the cylinder in order to force the piston downwards?

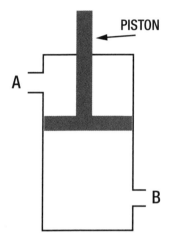

A. Point A

B. Point B

C. Both Point A and Point B

Answer

Question 16

At which point would you place the hook to keep the beam horizontal when lifted?

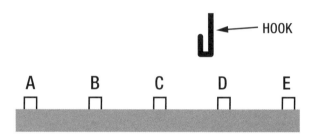

A. Point A

B. Point B

C. Point C

D. Point D

E. Point E

Answer

Question 17

At which point will the ball be travelling the fastest?

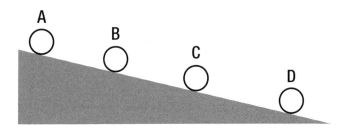

A. Point A

B. Point B

C. Point C

D. Point D

E. The same speed at each point

Answer [   ]

Question 18

If gear A moves to the right, which way will gear B move?

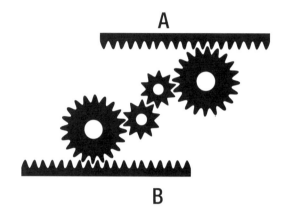

A. To the right

B. To the left

C. It won't move

D. Backwards and forward

Answer [   ]

Question 19

At which point will the beam balance?

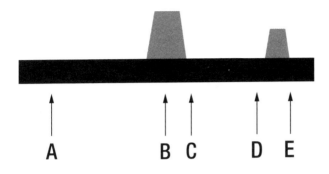

Answer [   ]

Question 20

Which is the heaviest load?

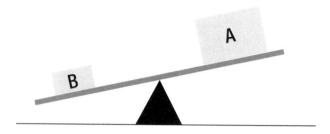

A. Load A

B. Load B

C. Both the same

Answer [   ]

Now that you have completed mechanical reasoning test 2, check your answers carefully before moving onto the next section of the guide.

ANSWERS TO MECHANICAL COMPREHENSION TEST 2

1. B

2. B

3. A

4. B

5. B

6. D

7. C

8. D

9. B

10. E

11. D

12. A

13. A

14. C

15. A

16. C

17. D

18. A

19. C

20. B

CHAPTER 7
THE NUMERICAL REASONING TEST

During the Royal Navy Recruiting Test you will also be required to sit a numerical reasoning test. The test itself consists of 30 questions and you have 16 minutes to complete it. The most effective way to prepare for the test is to carry out plenty of practice in relation to addition, subtraction, multiplication, division and also fractions, percentages and algebra.

During the real test you won't normally be permitted to use a calculator but you will be provided with a blank sheet of paper so that you can work out your answers. Within this section I have provided you with lots of sample test questions to help you prepare. Work carefully through the questions and be sure to check any you get wrong. There are 30 questions in this test and you have 16 minutes in which to answer them. Use a blank sheet of paper to work out the answers.

NUMERICAL REASONING TEST EXERCISE 1

Question 1

37 + ? = 95

A. 85   B. 45   C. 58   D. 57   E. 122

Answer [   ]

Question 2

86 - ? = 32

A. 54   B. 45   C. 108   D. 118   E. 68

Answer [   ]

Question 3

? + 104 = 210

A. 601   B. 314   C. 61   D.106   E.110

Answer [   ]

Question 4

109 x ? = 218

A. 1   B. 109   C. 12   D. 10   E. 2

Answer [   ]

how2become

Question 5

6 + 9 + 15 = 15 x ?

A. 15   B. 2   C. 3   D. 4   E. 5

Answer

Question 6

(34 + 13) − 4 = ? + 3

A. 7   B. 47   C. 51   D. 40   E. 37

Answer

Question 7

35 ÷ ? = 10 + 7.5

A. 2   B. 10   C. 4   D. 1   E. 17

Answer

Question 8

7 x ? = 28 x 3

A. 2   B. 3   C. 21   D. 15   E. 12

Answer

Question 9

100 ÷ 4 = 67 - ?

A. 42   B. 24   C. 57   D. 333   E. 2

Answer

Question 10

32 x 9 = 864 ÷ ?

A. 288   B. 3   C. 882   D. 4   E. None of
these

Answer

Question 11

**Following the pattern shown in the number sequence
below, what is the missing number?**

3   9   18   ?   72   144

A. 27   B. 36   C. 49   D. 21   E. 63

Answer

Question 12

**If you count from 1 to 100, how many 6s will you pass
on the way?**

A. 10   B. 19   C. 20   D. 11   E. 21

Answer

Question 13

50% of 350 = ?

A. 170   B. 25   C. 175   D. 170   E. 700

Answer

Question 14

75% of 1000 = ?

A.   75   B.   0.75   C.   75000   D.   750   E.
7.5

Answer

Question 15

40% of 40 = ?

A. 160   B.   4   C.   1600   D.   1.6   E.   16

Answer

Question 16

25% of 75 = ?

A. 18   B. 18.75   C. 18.25   D. 25   E. 17.25

Answer

Question 17

15% of 500 = ?

A. 75   B. 50   C. 0.75   D. 0.505   E. 750

Answer

Question 18

5% of 85 = ?

A. 4   B. 80   C. 4.25   D. 0.85   E. 89.25

Answer

Question 19

9876 – 6789 = ?

A. 3078   B. 3085   C. 783   D. 3086   E. 3087

Answer

Question 20

27 x 4 = ?

A. 106   B. 107   C. 108   D. 109   E. 110

Answer

Question 21

96 ÷ 4 = ?

A. 22   B. 23   C. 24   D. 25   E. 26

Answer [   ]

Question 22

8765 – 876 = ?

A. 9887   B. 7888   C. 7890   D. 7998   E. 7889

Answer [   ]

Question 23

623 + 222 = ?

A. 840   B. 845   C. 740   D. 745   E. 940

Answer [   ]

Question 24

A rectangle has an area of 24cm². The length of one side is 8cm. What is the perimeter of the rectangle?

A. 22 inches   B. 24cm   C. 18cm   D. 22cm   E. 18 inches

Answer [   ]

Question 25

**A square has a perimeter of 36cm. Its area is 81cm².
What is the length of one side?**

A. 9cm   B. 18cm   C. 9 metres   D. 18 metres   E. 16cm

Answer

Question 26

Which of the following is the same as 25/1000?

A. 0.25   B. 0.025   C. 0.0025   D. 40   E. 25000

Answer

Question 27

Is 33 divisible by 3?

A. Yes   B. No

Answer

Question 28

What is 49% of 1100?

A. 535   B. 536   C. 537   D. 538   E. 539

Answer

Question 29

One side of a rectangle is 12cm. If the area of the rectangle is 84cm², what is the length of shorter side?

A. 5cm   B. 6cm   C. 7cm   D. 8cm   E. 9cm

Answer

Question 30

A rectangle has an area of 8cm². The length of one side is 2cm. What is the perimeter?

A. 4cm   B. 6cm   C. 8cm   D. 10cm   E. None of these.

Answer

Now that you have completed the first numerical reasoning exercise, take the time to check through your answers carefully before moving on to exercise 2.

ANSWERS TO NUMERICAL REASONING TEST 1

1. C		**16.** B	
2. A		**17.** A	
3. D		**18.** C	
4. E		**19.** E	
5. B		**20.** C	
6. D		**21.** C	
7. A		**22.** E	
8. E		**23.** B	
9. A		**24.** D	
10. B		**25.** A	
11. B		**26.** B	
12. C		**27.** A	
13. C		**28.** E	
14. D		**29.** C	
15. E		**30.** E	

NUMERICAL REASONING TEST EXERCISE 2

There are 30 questions in this exercise and you have 16 minutes in which to answer them. Once again use a blank sheet of paper to work out the answers.

Question I

Calculate 5.99 + 16.02

A. 19.01

B. 20.01

C. 21.99

D. 22.99

E. 22.01

Answer

Question 2

Calculate 3.47 − 1.20

A. 22.7

B. 2.27

C. 1.27

D. 2.67

E. 0.27

Answer

Question 3

Calculate 98.26 – 62.89

A. 37.35

B. 35.37

C. 36.35

D. 36.37

E. 37.73

Answer

Question 4

Calculate 45.71 – 29.87

A. 14.84

B. 18.88

C. 14.89

D. 15.84

E. 15.85

Answer

Question 5

Calculate 564.87 + 321.60

A. 886.45

B. 886.74

C. 886.47

D. 868.47

E. 868.74

Answer

Question 6

Calculate 16.0 – 9.9

A. 6.9

B. 6.1

C. 7.1

D. 7.9

E. 5.1

Answer

Question 7

Calculate 1109.12 + 0.8

A. 1109.20

B. 1109.92

C. 1109.02

D. 1110.20

E. 1110.92

Answer

Question 8

Calculate 4.1 x 3.0

A. 123

B. 9.1

C. 12.41

D. 7.1

E. 12.3

Answer

Question 9

Calculate 16.8 x 4

A. 67.2

B. 64.8

C. 64.47.1

D. 67.4

E. 67.8

Answer

Question 10

Calculate 2.2 x 2.2

A. 4.4

B. 44.4

C. 2.84

D. 4.84

E. 8.44

Answer

Question II

In the following question what is the value of t?

$$\frac{5\,(t - 32)}{2} = 5$$

A. 64

B. 128

C. 43

D. 34

E. 39

Answer

Question I2

In the following question what is the value of t?

$$\frac{3\,(t + 35)}{6} = 35$$

A. 35

B. 70

C. 75

D. 77

E. 30

Answer

Question 13

In the following question what is the value of t?

$$\frac{9 \, (t \times 16)}{5} = 144$$

A. 6

B. 3

C. 9

D. 15

E. 5

Answer [   ]

Question 14

In the following question what is the value of t?

$$\frac{4t - 16}{32} = 2$$

A. 5

B. 10

C. 15

D. 20

E. 25

Answer [   ]

Question 15

Convert 0.7 to a fraction.

A. $\frac{7}{10}$

B. $\frac{3}{4}$

C. $\frac{75}{1}$

D. $\frac{1}{10}$

E. $\frac{2}{3}$

Answer

Question 16

Convert 2.5 to a fraction.

A. $\frac{25}{1}$

B. $\frac{3}{6}$

C. $2\frac{1}{2}$

D. $\frac{1}{25}$

E. $2\frac{2}{1}$

Answer

Question 17

Convert 3.75 to a fraction.

A. $\frac{75}{1}$

B. $\frac{1}{375}$

C. $3\frac{1}{75}$

D. $\frac{75}{3}$

E. $3\frac{3}{4}$

Answer

Question 18

Convert ³⁄₁₀ to a decimal.

A. 3.0

B. 0.3

C. 3.33

D. 0.03

E. 0.003

Answer [   ]

Question 19

Convert ¼ to a decimal.

A. 0.025

B. 2.5

C. 0.25

D. 0.4

E. 4.0

Answer [   ]

Question 20

Convert ⅘ to a decimal.

A. 0.08

B. 8.0

C. 4.5

D. 5.4

E. 0.8

Answer [   ]

Question 21

60 x 0.25 = ?

A. 125

B. 20

C. 15

D. 10

E. 5

Answer

Question 22

The clock below reads 10:10 am. How many degrees will the large (minute) hand have turned when the time reaches 11:10 am?

A. 60°

B. 360°

C. 90°

D. 180°

E. 12°

Answer

Question 23

The clock below reads 10:10 am. How many degrees will the large (minute) hand have turned when the time reaches 10:55 am

A. 45°

B. 360°

C. 90°

D. 180°

E. 270°

Answer

Question 24

The clock below reads 10:10 am. How many degrees will the small (hour) hand have turned when the time reaches 4:10 pm?

A. 60°

B. 360°

C. 90°

D. 180°

E. 270°

Answer

Question 25

220 x 0.75 = ?

A. 110

B. 180

C. 200

D. 160

E. 165

Answer

Question 26

What is the number 67.987651 correct to 3 decimal places?

A. 67.988

B. 68

C. 67.987

D. 67.9

E. 67.98

Answer

Question 27

What is the number 88.88087 correct to 2 decimal places?

A. 89.0

B. 89.9

C. 88.90

D. 88.88

E. 89.88

Answer _____

Question 28

550 x 0.2 = ?

A. 110

B. 100

C. 50

D. 55

E. 275

Answer _____

Question 29

1100 x 0.3 = ?

A. 90

B. 300

C. 990

D. 330

E. 310

Answer [   ]

Question 30
890 x 0.4 = ?

A. 890.4

B. 356

C. 8904

D. 365

E. 445

Answer [   ]

Now that you have completed numerical reasoning test exercise 2, take the time to carefully work through your answers. Make sure you learn from any mistakes you made.

ANSWERS TO NUMERICAL REASONING TEST 2

1. E	**16.** C
2. B	**17.** E
3. B	**18.** B
4. D	**19.** C
5. C	**20.** E
6. B	**21.** C
7. B	**22.** B
8. E	**23.** E
9. A	**24.** D
10. D	**25.** E
11. D	**26.** A
12. A	**27.** D
13. E	**28.** A
14. D	**29.** D
15. A	**30.** B

FINAL TIPS FOR PASSING THE ROYAL NAVY RECRUITING TEST

- In the build up to the test make sure you get in plenty of practice in the assessable areas.

- Carry out 'deliberate' and 'repetitive' practice and work hard on your weak areas in order to improve. This effectively means concentrating harder on your weaker areas, and doing everything you can to improve.

- Practise under timed conditions and without the aid of a calculator. Use a blank sheet of paper to work out your calculations.

- If you find that you are struggling to understand the practice tests then consider getting some personal tuition or help.

- Drink plenty of water in the build up to the tests in order to maintain your concentration levels.

- Practise little and often as opposed to 'cramming' the night before the test.

CHAPTER 8
HOW TO PASS THE ROYAL MARINES COMMANDO INTERVIEW

INTRODUCTION

During this section of the guide I will provide you with a number of tips and advice on how to pass the Royal Marines Commando interview. The information will be relevant for both the Armed Forces Career Office (AFCO) interview and the Potential Royal Marines Course (PRMC) interview.

The Royal Marines will assess you against a broad range of criteria. Before I provide you with sample interview questions and responses, I will explain the different areas that you need to focus on during your preparation for the interview. The criteria that I am going to provide you with during this section of the guide relate to your own personal attributes, qualities and also your knowledge of the Royal Marines

and your chosen career. This information will act as a very good foundation for your preparation. If you are capable of providing the selecting officers with what they are looking for then your chances of success will greatly increase.

The marking sheet used to assess your abilities covers a number of different assessable areas. The following list is a selection of some of the criteria used:

• Personal turnout;

• Sociability;

• Emotional maturity and stability;

• Drive and determination to succeed;

• Physically robust;

• Experience of being self-reliant;

• Reactions to social discipline;

• Experience of and reaction to regimentation and routine;

• Knowledge and experience of Royal Marines life;

• Motivation to join the Royal Marines;

• Personal circumstances.

This list is not exhaustive and there will be other areas that the Royal Marines will be assessing you on during the interviews and written tests. However, having an understanding of the qualities you need to demonstrate throughout selection will improve your chances of success dramatically.

In order to provide you with a greater understanding of what is required I will now go into more detail about each specific area.

PERSONAL TURNOUT

The Royal Marines are looking for you to be smartly dressed when you attend the AFCO. This should be for every visit. During my research I spoke to a number of recruiting officers at various AFCOs and the general consensus was that they would expect applicants to dress smartly for every visit, not just the interview. They want to see that you have made an effort to present yourself positively. When you attend the careers office, whether it is for an interview or a careers presentation, always make sure you wear a formal outfit such as a suit or shirt and tie. I believe this is very important if you are to gain higher marks in the area of 'personal turnout'.

Many people will stroll into the careers office wearing jeans and trainers. Make an effort to stand out for the right reasons and this certainly will work in your favour. Those people who turn up to the Armed Forces Careers Office unwashed and dressed untidily will score poorly. Throughout the duration of the guide I will make reference to the importance of dressing smartly and making the effort to present yourself in a positive, motivated and professional manner.

Tips for scoring high in personal turnout
• Make sure your shoes are clean and polished;

• Shirt, trousers and tie should be worn for every visit;

• Ensure your clothes are ironed and not creased;

• Work on your personal hygiene and overall appearance. Make sure your nails are clean!

• Stand tall and be confident;

• Don't slouch in the interview chair.

SOCIABILITY

This section assesses your ability to mix well with people. As you can imagine, Royal Marines are extremely confident and sociable people. They need to be in order to carry out the job they do. Teamwork is a very important aspect of their work, so there is no room for people who are either loners or prefer to work on their own. The Royal Marines want to know that you are socially confident and outgoing. It is also important that you have a good sense of humour. They want to know that you can fit in well with the Marines way of life and that you have no problems with communal living.

When you join the Royal Marines you will be required to live in accommodation that houses many people. As you progress up through the ranks the amount of people you'll be required to live with will decrease, until you eventually get a room on your own! Some people find it very difficult to socialise with others and these are not the type of people the service want to recruit. They need people who will fit into the team spirit and who have no problem with communicating with others. Those applicants who come across as quiet or shy will not score well in the area of sociability. At no point during selection should you be brash, abrasive or not a team player.

Tips for scoring high in sociability
• During the interviews provide examples of where you have mixed well with others. This may be through youth organisations such as the Scouts, or football/rugby teams;

• If you have played team sports then this will be an advantage. If you don't currently play team sports then I recommend that you start now!

• Tell the interviewer that you will have no problem with

communal living. Communal living is living with other people. You may be in a room of up to thirty other people during your training, so they want to know that you are comfortable with this. If you can provide examples of where you have lived with others then this will be an advantage;

• Smile and laugh where appropriate – a sense of humour is a must but never be overbearing or overconfident. Never 'backchat' or be disrespectful to the recruiting officers at the AFCO and staff at the PRMC.

EMOTIONAL MATURITY AND STABILITY

The Royal Marines want to see that you are mature for your age and that you are even-tempered and well-balanced. They don't want people who are aggressive or who come across with a bad attitude. They want to see that you have coped well with the ups and downs of life so far and you may find that they ask you questions on any difficult areas of life that you have had to deal with. They want to know that you will adapt well to the change in lifestyle when you join the Marines and that you can cope in highly stressful situations. They will also be looking for you to be mature for your age and that there are no signs of depression or anxiety. They will also be assessing your ability to cope well with unfamiliar surroundings and that you will not become homesick during training.

Tips for scoring high in emotional maturity and stability
• During the interviews and during discussions with the Armed Forces Careers Officer, try to provide examples of where you have dealt well with difficult situations in your life in a positive and mature manner;

 how2become

• Try to be upbeat and positive about the future;

• Don't be overconfident or macho.

DRIVE AND DETERMINATION TO SUCCEED

During the interview the assessor will want to see evidence that you have a sense of purpose to your life. They will be looking for a pattern of achievement, either through school or at work, and for evidence that you are not easily deflected from your goals and aspirations. They want to see that you are a competitive person who is highly motivated to succeed. Having drive and determination means that you have the ability to keep working hard and improving yourself until you achieve success.

Those applicants who show signs that they give up easily or have no goals and aspirations will score poorly in the area of drive and determination to succeed.

Tips for scoring high in drive and determination to succeed

• Provide examples of where you have achieved. This might be educational qualifications, courses that you have attended or even sporting achievements;

• Be positive about joining the Royal Marines and tell them that nothing is going to stop you from succeeding. Remember that it is extremely tough to pass selection, so you will need to persuade them that you have what it takes to succeed;

• Demonstrate that your ambition and sense of purpose is to join the Royal Marines and become a professional and competent soldier.

PHYSICALLY ROBUST

It is crucial that you are involved in either outdoor activities and/or team sports – and I don't mean cricket! Being physically active is important and if you are strong and free from injuries and weakness then this will be an advantage during selection. If you are not involved in any form of team sports then I advise that you start straight away. It is very easy to become involved in team sports, as there are so many to choose from. Examples of team sports include football and rugby.

Those applicants who provide evidence that they are generally isolated individuals who spend too much time at home on the computer or watching TV will score lower than those who are physically active.

Tips for scoring high in physical robustness

• Be involved in competitive team sports;

• Be an active outdoor type of person;

• Attend the gym and carry out light weight exercises and workouts.

EXPERIENCE OF BEING SELF-RELIANT

Do you think you can handle the pressure of living away from home? Or better still, can you provide evidence of where you have already done this? If you have travelled or have been on camps where you have had to 'rough it' then this would certainly be an advantage. Basically, they want to know that you can look after yourself without the help of your parents or home comforts.

If you have no experience whatsoever of being self-reliant

then I advise that you take steps to improve your experience of this area. For example, there is nothing to stop you from going camping for the weekend or joining the Cadets, where you will be able to gain experience of this important attribute.

Tips for scoring high in being self-reliant

• Provide examples of where you have been away from home for short or long periods of time;

• Tell the interviewer that you enjoy travelling and being away from home. Remember that it is important to provide examples of where you have already done this.

• Tell the interviewer that you are looking forward to leaving home to join the Royal Marines and face the challenges that it presents;

• Provide examples of where you have had to fend for yourself or where you have been away camping.

REACTIONS TO SOCIAL DISCIPLINE

The Royal Marines want to see that you have a positive attitude towards authority. People in authority include the police, your parents, teachers and even your boss at work. When you join the service you will be taking orders from senior officers and they want to know that you have no problem with authority.

There is a strong possibility that the interviewer will ask you questions that relate to your attitude to education and your teachers. At no point should you be negative about your teachers or about people who are in positions of authority. If you are disrespectful or negative about these people then there is a strong possibility that the selection officers will take a dim view on your attitude. For example, I have been

aware of applicants who complain during the interview that their teachers were rubbish at their job and that everyone in the class would always laugh at them. As you can imagine, those applicants do not progress any further during the selection process.

Tips for scoring high in social discipline

• Try to provide examples of where you have carried out orders, either at work or at school;

• Tell the interviewer that you respect authority, providing you do of course, and that you see it as an important aspect of life. You do not have a problem with taking orders from anyone, including people who are the opposite sex to you.

EXPERIENCE OF AND REACTION TO REGIMENTATION AND ROUTINE

When you join the Royal Marines you will lose much of your personal freedom. During your initial training there will be many restrictions placed upon you in terms of leave and your general freedom. You won't be given the time to do all of the things that you usually do whilst at home. Therefore, the interviewer will want to see that you have the ability to cope with this added pressure and disciplined routine.

You must try to demonstrate during the selection process that you have already experienced some form of routine and that you are capable of following rules and regulations. This could simply be by having some form of disciplined routine at home, whereby you are required to clean the house and carry out the ironing for a few hours every week.

Tips for scoring high in experience of and reaction to regimentation and routine

- Provide examples of where you have lost your personal freedom, either during your upbringing, at school or during work. Maybe you have had to work unsociable hours or had to dedicate time and effort to your educational studies?

- Tell the interviewer that you fully understand that you will lose your personal freedom when you join the Royal Marines and that it won't be a problem for you.

- Implement some form of routine into your preparation strategy for joining the Marines. Set out your action plan early on and follow it rigidly.

KNOWLEDGE AND EXPERIENCE OF THE ROYAL MARINES

Having knowledge of the Royal Marines can be achieved in a number of ways. If you have been a member of any youth organisations then this will be an obvious advantage. Youth organisations include the Scouts, Army Cadets, Air Training Corps or Sea Cadets etc. If a member of your family or a friend is a member of the Armed Forces then you can also gain knowledge through them, simply by asking them questions about their job and life within the Armed Forces. It is also important to gain knowledge by reading your recruitment literature and visiting the Royal Marines website if you have access to the internet. I would also strongly recommend that you try to visit a Royal Marines establishment. This can normally be achieved by speaking to your Armed Forces Careers Liaison Officer.

Tips for scoring high in knowledge and experience of the Royal Marines

- Speak to any friends or relatives who are members of the Armed Forces and ask them what it is like. Gain as much information as possible from the Armed Forces Careers Office staff and also through your recruitment literature;

- Find out as much as possible about the training you will undertake when you join the Royal Marines for your chosen career and also your initial recruit training;

- Consider visiting an establishment or museum. These are great places to learn about the Royal Marines;

- Consider joining a youth organisation such as the Scouts or Cadets to gain some experience of a disciplined service.

MOTIVATION TO JOIN THE ROYAL MARINES

The interviewer will want to see that it is your own decision to join and that you haven't been pushed into it by friends or your family. They want to see that you have been pulled by the attractions of the Royal Marines as opposed to being pushed into them. If you are successful in your application then they will be investing a tremendous amount of time, energy and finances into your training and development. The last thing they want is for you to decide it's not for you.

Tips for scoring high in motivation to join the Royal Marines

- Always present a positive attitude towards joining when you visit the Armed Forces Careers Office and also whilst attending the PRMC. This choice of career should be something that you have considered very carefully and you have been working very hard to make sure that you pass;

- Try to think about what attracts you to the Royal Marines and tell the interviewer during selection.

PERSONAL CIRCUMSTANCES

The interviewer will want to know that you have the support of your family and/or your partner. They also want to see that you are free from any detracting circumstances such as financial difficulties. If you are in financial difficulty then this could have a negative effect on your mental health during training. They will assess your personal circumstances during selection and also at the PRMC interview.

Tips for scoring high in personal circumstances

• Speak to your parents and your partner (if applicable) about your choice of career. Ask them for their support;

• If they do not support you or they are concerned about you joining then I would recommend that you take them along to the careers office so that the Army Forces Careers Officer can talk to them about Royal Marines life and answer any questions that they may have. It is imperative that you have their full support.

On the following pages I have provided you with sample interview questions and sample responses to help you prepare. I have also indicated areas that you may wish to research in order to find the answers to these questions. Remember, these questions are generic and they should be used as a preparation tool only. They are not guaranteed to be the exact questions you'll be asked during your selection interview, although they will be very similar.

After each interview question I advise that you create your own response, using a blank sheet of paper, based on your own qualities and attributes.

The following is a list of areas you may be asked questions on during the selection interview:

- The reasons why you want to join the Royal Marines.

- What information you already know about the Royal Marines, its history, lifestyle and training.

- About your hobbies and interests including sporting activities.

- Your personal responsibilities.

- Your achievements to date.

- Information about your family and what they think about you joining. Do they support you?

- Information based around your application form.

- Your experience of work and education and whether you had/have any responsibilities at work.

- Your emotional stability and your maturity.

- Your drive and determination to succeed.

- Having a positive reaction to the disciplined environment.

- Your knowledge of life within the Royal Marines.

- Questions surrounding your application.

SAMPLE INTERVIEW QUESTION NUMBER 1

Why do you want to join the Royal Marines?

This is an almost guaranteed question and one that you should be prepared for. Think hard about the reasons why you want to become a Royal Marines Commando. What has attracted you to the job? Do you know what the job involves? Have you carried out sufficient research? Remember that the Royal Marines want to know if candidates have the

determination, physical fitness, stamina, mental ability, cool headedness and the ability to rise to a challenge. The Royal Marines have an amazing history of achievement and pride themselves on being the elite of all the Armed Forces.

Take a look at the following sample response before using a blank sheet of paper to prepare your own.

SAMPLE RESPONSE NUMBER 1

Why do you want to join the Royal Marines?

'I have wanted to join the Royal Marines for a number of years now and feel that I have now reached a point in my life where I am ready to commit to the service. Having studied the Royal Marines recruitment literature and visited the Royal Navy website I am impressed by the professionalism and standards the service sets itself.

I fully understand that the training is very difficult and I have been working hard to prepare myself for the challenge. The Royal Marines have a fantastic history of achievement and I want to be part of this elite service. I am a determined, focused and driven person who rises to any challenge and the Royal Marines is a career that I want. The Royal Marines undertake any kind of military or security job under any conditions anywhere in the world at a moment's notice and I believe that I can bring something to the team. Yes, I know that I will have to work very hard to pass both the PRMC and the 30-week course but I will make sure that I am fully prepared.'

SAMPLE INTERVIEW QUESTION NUMBER 2

What does your family think of you wanting to join the Royal Marines?

Again, you are likely to be asked a question surrounding your family background and what they think about you wanting to join. It is important that your family support you in your decision. If they have any doubts about you joining the service then you may wish to consider taking them to the Royal Navy careers office so they can ask any questions or raise concerns that they may have. When answering questions such as this it is important that you are honest and tell the truth. If your family have any concerns then share them with the careers officer. They will then be able to advise you on the best way for your family/partner to overcome any fears they may have.

There now follows a sample response to this question to help you prepare. However, this question must be answered based solely on your own individual circumstances.

SAMPLE RESPONSE NUMBER 2

What does your family think of you wanting to join the Royal Marines?

'I have discussed the issue with them in depth and also shown them all of the recruitment literature to try to dampen any fears that they may have. They were concerned about me joining but they gave me their full support after I explained to them everything I know about the training I will go through and the conditions I will serve under. They are aware that the Royal Marines has a very difficult training course but they fully support me and they have been impressed by how much work I have been putting into my preparation. They know how determined I am to succeed.

They have seen how enthusiastic I am about joining the Royal Marines and know that I will make a great member of this

team. I have also discussed the issue with my partner and he/she is extremely supportive. They are all looking forward to, hopefully, seeing me at my passing out parade if I am successful and therefore I have their full backing.'

SAMPLE INTERVIEW QUESTION NUMBER 3

How do you think you will cope with the Royal Marines way of life in relation to the discipline and being part of a military organisation?

When you join the Royal Marines you will be joining a military organisation that has set procedures, standards and discipline codes. To some people this will come as a shock and the Royal Marines want to know that you are prepared for this change in lifestyle. They are investing time, effort and resources in your training so they want to know that you can cope with their way of life.

When answering this type of question you need to demonstrate both your awareness of what the Royal Marines life involves and also your positive attitude towards the disciplined environment. Study the recruitment literature and visit the careers website to get a feel for the type of training you will be going through.

SAMPLE RESPONSE NUMBER 3

How do you think you will cope with the Royal Marines way of life in relation to the discipline and being part of a military organisation?

'Having read the information available to me about the Royal Marines, I think I would cope very well. I know that I will find it difficult at times but believe I have both the maturity and

stability to succeed and become a competent member of the team.

I have a level head and I have the ability to rise to any challenge so I feel that I would not have any problem with discipline. I have always respected authority, both in society, at work and also when I was in education. Discipline is very important and without it the service would not function effectively. The very nature of the Commando's role means that the service requires a disciplined workforce. Without that discipline things can go wrong. If I am successful and do not carry out my duties professionally then I could endanger somebody's life. I understand why discipline is required and believe I would cope with it well. I understand that being in the Royal Marines isn't a 9-5 job but instead you are required to take on tasks whenever required.'

SAMPLE INTERVIEW QUESTION NUMBER 4

How do you think you will cope with being away from home and losing your personal freedom?

This type of question is one that needs to be answered positively.

There is only one correct answer to this question and you need to demonstrate that you have considered the consequences of leaving home and are fully aware of what is involved.

If you have any experience of being away from home then you should state this in your response. Try to think of occasions when you have been away for periods of time and tell the interviewers that it wasn't an issue. Have you ever been a part of any youth organisations? If you have then this will undoubtedly go in your favour. Giving an example is far better than just saying you will be able to cope.

Take a look at the following sample response and try to structure your response around this.

SAMPLE RESPONSE NUMBER 4

How do you think you will cope with being away from home and losing your personal freedom?

'Having had experience of being away from home, I believe I would cope extremely well. When I was younger I was a member of the Scouts and I often went away for expeditions at weekends. Even now I am always looking for any excuse to get away from home. I love the outdoors and often visit the Lake District, where I go camping, running and hill climbing. Being away from home has never bothered me and this would certainly not be an issue for me.

In fact I am looking forward to leaving home!'

SAMPLE INTERVIEW QUESTION NUMBER 5

Are you involved in any sporting activities and how do you keep yourself fit?

When answering questions based around your own physical fitness you need to be honest, but also bear in mind the following points:

- Although you don't have to be super fit to join the Royal Marines, you do need to have a good all-round level of physical fitness, so being fit in the first instance is important.

- The Royal Marines, just like any of the services, pride themselves on their ability to work as an effective team unit. Those people who engage in active team sports

are more likely to be competent team members. If you play a team sport then this will be a good thing to tell the interview panel. If you don't then it may be a good idea to go and join one!

Regardless of the above points remember that if you don't do any physical activity whatsoever then you will score low in this area. Make sure you partake in some form of physical activity.

SAMPLE RESPONSE NUMBER 5

Are you involved in any sporting activities and how do you keep yourself fit?

'Yes I am. I currently play in the local rugby team and have been doing that for a number of years now. Maintaining a good level of fitness is something I enjoy. In fact recently I have increased my fitness levels by going swimming 3 times a week in the evenings. I'm aware that during the recruitment training course I will be pushed to my limits so I need to be prepared for that. I believe the fact that I play team sports will help me get through my training.

I also work out at the gym doing light weights work. In the mornings before I go to work I get up at 6am and go running five miles. This sets me up for the day and also keeps my fitness levels at a good standard. I understand that during the 30-week course I will be pushed to my limits so I have been preparing for this for the last 4 months.'

SAMPLE INTERVIEW QUESTION NUMBER 6

How do you think you will fit into a team environment?

Once again it would be a positive thing if you can demonstrate

you have experience of working in a team. Maybe you have experience of working in a sporting team or need to work in a team in your part-time job? Try to think of examples where you have already been working in a team environment and if you can provide an example where the team actually achieved something, then that's even better.

Structure your answer around your own experiences and also around your knowledge of the fact that the Royal Marines need to work as an effective team unit in order to complete their tasks both safely and on time.

SAMPLE RESPONSE NUMBER 6

How do you think you will fit into a team environment?

'I have had experience of working in a team and I really enjoyed it so I know I would fit in well. I play for my local rugby team and it is important that everybody gels together to try to win our games. The real test for the team is when we are being beaten and I always try to rally the team together and get us motivated to win back the points we have lost. I understand that the Royal Marines need to work together effectively as a team to get the right result. If the team doesn't perform then people's lives can be put at risk. I know that as a Royal Marine I won't just be acting with the other men in my team, I will be thinking with them too.

Being an effective part of the team also means that I would have to train hard and keep up my competency levels, which I believe I would do well. With my experience of team sports and having the ability to pull a team together when the chips are down, I think I would be a great asset to the Royal Marines.'

SAMPLE INTERVIEW QUESTION NUMBER 7

What do you do in your spare time?

With questions of this nature the Royal Marines recruitment staff are looking to see if you use your leisure time wisely. This will tell them a lot about your attitude, motivation and determination to succeed.

We all know that some people spend their spare time doing nothing or watching TV and playing computer games. When you join the Royal Marines you won't have much time to do nothing so they want you tell them that you are active and that you are doing worthwhile things. For example, if you are involved in any sports, outdoor activities or are part of any youth organisation such as the Sea Cadets then these are good things to tell them. You may also be involved in voluntary work or charity work and once again these will work well for you. If you currently do very little with your spare time then now is a good time to make a lifestyle change. Embark on a fitness routine or join an activity club or organisation.

SAMPLE RESPONSE NUMBER 7

What do you do in your spare time?

'During my spare time I like to keep active, both physically and mentally. I enjoy visiting the gym 3 times a week and I have a structured workout, which I try to vary every 3 months to keep my interest up. I am a very active/outdoor person and often go off for weekends camping and hill walking.

I'm also a keen rugby player and play for my local side every weekend during the rugby season. We usually train once a week too, which allows us to concentrate on our team skills and also on improving our weaker areas and general fitness.

I'm also a member of the local Sea Cadet force, which is an evening's commitment every week and the occasional weekend. Of course, I know when it is time to relax and usually do this by either listening to music or playing snooker with my friends but overall I'm a very active person. I certainly don't like sitting around doing nothing. I understand that if I'm successful in joining the Royal Marines there will be plenty of things to do in the evenings to keep me occupied such as using the gym and study time.'

SAMPLE INTERVIEW QUESTION NUMBER 8

Can you tell us about any personal achievements you have experienced during your life so far?

Having achieved something in your life demonstrates that you have the ability to see things through to the end. It also shows that you are motivated and determined to succeed. The Royal Marines want to see evidence that you can achieve, as there is a greater chance of you completing the initial recruit course if you have a history of this. Try to think of examples where you have succeeded or achieved something relevant in your life.

Some good examples of achievements are as follows:

- Duke of Edinburgh Awards;

- A levels or educational qualifications;

- Team or individual sports awards, trophies and medals;

- Raising money for charity.

Obviously you'll have your own achievements that you will want to add into your response, but use the following sample response as a guide.

SAMPLE RESPONSE NUMBER 8

Can you tell us about any personal achievements you have experienced during your life so far?

'So far in my life I have managed to achieve a number of things that I am proud of. To begin with, I recently worked hard to achieve my GCSE results, which enabled me to go on to further education and study my choice of subject. Without these grades I would not have been able to do that.

About a year ago the football team that I play in won the league trophy for the second year running, which is another one of my more recent achievements. However, my most memorable achievement to date is managing to raise £1,000 for a local charity. I worked hard and ran a marathon in order to raise the money. I was particularly proud of this achievement because It meant the charity I ran for were able to purchase some important items of equipment that could be used to treat some of their patients.'

SAMPLE INTERVIEW QUESTION NUMBER 9

What are your strengths?

This is a common interview question, which is relatively easy to answer. The problem with it is that many people use the same response. It is quite an easy thing to tell the interviewer that you are dedicated and the right person for the job. However, it is a different thing backing it up with evidence! If you are asked this type of question make sure you are positive during your response and show that you actually mean what you are saying. Then back it up with examples of when you have done something that you say you are proud of. For example, if you tell the panel that you are a motivated person then you should also tell them about an event in

your life where you achieved something through motivation and determination.

SAMPLE RESPONSE NUMBER 9

What are your strengths?

'To begin with, I'm a determined person who likes to see things through to the end. For example I recently ran a marathon for charity. I'd never done this kind of thing before and found it very hard work but I made sure I completed the task.

Another strength of mine is that I'm always looking for ways to improve myself. As an example, I was preparing for the Royal Marines selection process by performing mock academic tests. I noticed that I was getting a number of questions wrong so in order to improve I decided to get some personal tuition at my college to ensure that I could pass this part of the test.

Finally I would say that one of my biggest strengths is that I'm a great team player. I really enjoy working in a team environment and achieving things through a collaborative approach. For example, I play in a local rugby team and we recently won the league trophy for the first time since the club was established some 50 years ago.'

SAMPLE INTERVIEW QUESTION NUMBER 10

What is your biggest weakness?

Now there's a question! If we were all totally honest with ourselves we could probably write a whole list of weaknesses. Now I wouldn't advise that you reel off a whole list of weaknesses in your interview as you could do yourself

a lot of harm. Conversely, those people who say that they don't have any weaknesses are lying!

If you are asked a question of this nature then it is important that you give at least one weakness. The trick here is to make the weakness sound like a strength. For example, a person may say that one of their weaknesses is that their own personal standards are too high sometimes and they expect this of others. Or another one is that a person doesn't know when to relax. They are always on the go achieving and making things happen when they should take more time out to relax and recuperate. Take a look at the following sample response before using a blank sheet of paper to prepare your own response.

SAMPLE RESPONSE NUMBER 10

What is your biggest weakness?

'That's a difficult question but I know that I do have a particular weakness. The standards that I always set myself are quite high and unfortunately I get frustrated when other people's aren't. For example, I am hardly ever late for anything and believe that punctuality is important. However, if I'm left waiting for other people who are late I usually have to say something to them when they finally arrive, which isn't always a good thing. I need to understand that not everyone's the same, and I need to let some things go over my head.'

SAMPLE INTERVIEW QUESTION NUMBER 11

Can you tell me what you have learnt about the Royal Marines basic training?

This type of question is designed to see how much knowledge

you have of the basic training you will go through if you are successful. If you have no idea what training involves then there is a higher risk that you will not successfully finish the course. Information about the Royal Marines basic training can be found in your recruitment literature and also by visiting the Royal Navy careers website, which can be found at www.royalnavy.mod.uk.

There now follows a sample response to this question. Once you have read it, take the time to carry out some research and construct your own response using a blank sheet of paper.

SAMPLE RESPONSE NUMBER 11

Can you tell me what you have learnt about the Royal Marines basic training?

'If I am successful during the selection process and the PRMC I will go to CTRM at Lympstone and start the 30-week course. There will be up to 60 other recruits at the beginning of the course. During the 30-week course I will learn the meaning of the word teamwork, learn how to react speedily to unpredictable situations, learn how to be smart and have good bearing, and understand the responsibilities of being a serviceman and upholding the reputation of the Royal Marines.

The 30-week course is split up into 7 different sections.

Section 1 is the foundation course, which is three weeks in total. This involves admin, drill and physical training. Section 2 is six weeks long and involves weapons training, map reading and exercises. Section 3 is four weeks long and is advanced skills training. Section 4 is seven weeks in total and is operations of war training. Section 5 is a two-week

commando course. Section 6 is professional training and the final 30th week is King's Squad, which is drill and pre-leave admin.'

SAMPLE INTERVIEW QUESTION NUMBER 12

What do you know about the history of the Royal Marines?

During the interview, either at the Careers Office or at the PRMC, you will be asked a question that relates to your knowledge of the Royal Marines history. Within your Royal Marines recruitment literature you will find a section that covers the history of the service. Make sure you read it!

Knowing a little bit about the history of the Royal Marines is a good thing and it demonstrates that you have taken the time to learn about the roll call of daring deeds and valiant victories. Once you have read the history pages in your recruitment literature, read the following sample response before creating your own answer using a blank sheet of paper.

SAMPLE RESPONSE NUMBER 12

What do you know about the history of the Royal Marines?

'The Royal Marines history stems back over 335 years in total and began during the reign of Charles II. One of the most significant battles was that of Gibraltar in 1704, where the Royal Marines held out for eight months whilst under siege. The Gibraltar is the only battle honour worn in the badge and the colours. Throughout the years the Royal Marines have fought and won in many battles ranging from the Seven Years War through to the more recent Falkland Islands in 1982.

Other battles of interest include the Glorious First of June in

1794, the capture of Canton in 1841, the siege of Sevastopol in 1854, the Boer War and both the First and Second World Wars.'

SAMPLE INTERVIEW QUESTION NUMBER 13

What can you tell me about the badge of the Royal Marines?

Whilst this type of question may not come up during your interview, we recommend that you take the time to familiarise yourself with the different elements of the badge. The reason for this is that it will show the recruitment officer that you have taken your research that one step further. It will show that you are serious about the Royal Marines and that you have taken an interest in where they have come from and how they have been formed over the years.

There now follows a sample response to this question with a brief explanation to each part of the Royal Marines badge. Take your time to absorb the information and learn each part of the badge before using a blank sheet of paper to construct your own response to this question.

SAMPLE RESPONSE NUMBER 13

What can you tell me about the badge of the Royal Marines?

THE LION AND CROWN *- This identifies that the regiment is of 'royal' standing. This honour was conferred in 1802 by George III.*

GIBRALTAR *- The capture and defence of Gibraltar in 1704 is highly significant in the history of the Royal Marines. Because of this George IV decided that it should be a part of the Royal Marines badge.*

THE GLOBE - *The globe was chosen by George IV as it represented the success of the Royal Marines in every corner of the world.*

PER MARE PER TERRAM - *This is the motto of the Royal Marines and was first used in 1775. It means 'By Sea by Land'.*

Over the next few pages I will provide you with further sample interview questions and responses.

OTHER COMMON QUESTIONS AND ANSWERS

Q14. What is the date of birth of the Corps?

A. 28th October 1664.

Q15. What is the motto of the Royal Marines?

A. Per Mare Per Terram.

Q16. What does the motto mean?

A. By Sea By Land.

Q17. Describe the Corps Badge

A. The Lion and Crown denotes a 'Royal' regiment. George III conferred this honour in 1802 'in consideration of the very meritorious services of the Marines in the late war'. The Great Globe itself, surrounded by laurels, was chosen by George IV as a symbol of the Marines' successes in every quarter of the world. The laurels are believed to honour the gallantry they displayed during the capture of Belle Isle in 1761. 'Gibraltar' represents the capture and defence of that territory in 1704. It was considered by George IV to be one of the most glorious achievements of the Royal Marines and he decided that the words should represent the honours

they had earned. The Fouled Anchor, incorporated into the emblem in 1747, is the badge of the Lord High Admiral and shows that the Corps is part of the Royal Navy. 'Per Mare Per Terram', 'By Sea By Land', is the motto of the Royal Marines, believed to have been used for the first time in 1785.

Q18. What happened at Walcheren?

A. The Assault on Walcheren took place on the 1st of November 1944. The leading troops in the successful seaborne attack on Walcheren in November 1944, were the 4th Special Service Brigade (Brigadier B W Leicester DSO) consisting of Numbers 41, 47 and 48 Commandos and Number 4 Army Commando. The three RM Commandos attacked Westkapelle, to open Antwerp Port. This was the first amphibious assault carried out by the Royal Marines.

Q19. Who was Hannah Snell?

A. In late 1747, the young Worcester born Hannah Snell dressed herself in men's clothes and enlisted with the Marines at Portsmouth. Under the name of James Gray, she sailed to India as part of a large expedition sent to capture the French occupied town of Pondicherry. While in the East, Snell fought in two sieges and claims to have received many injuries, including a bullet wound to her groin. Despite these injuries and her close proximity to her shipmates, she says she concealed her true sex until her return to England in early 1750. Eager to profit from her adventures, Snell immediately sold her story to the London publisher, Robert Walker. Her appearance on stage in uniform caused a sensation and news of her adventures quickly spread across the country. In November 1750, the Royal Chelsea Hospital officially recognised Snell's military service and granted her a lifetime pension. She lived for another 40 years, marrying twice and

raising two boys. In 1791, Snell was admitted to the notorious Bedlam lunatic asylum, where she died six months later.

Q20. Who is the Commandant General of the Royal Marines?

A. Major General Andy Salmon CMG OBE RM (correct at time of writing)

Q21. What are the 3 Commando units called?

A. 40 Commando Royal Marines, 42 Commando Royal Marines, 45 Commando Royal Marines.

Q22. Where are the Commando units Located?

A. 40 Commando - Norton Manor Camp, Taunton.

42 Commando – Bickleigh Barracks, Plymouth.

45 Commando - RM Condor, Arbroath.

Q23. Name five of the specialist qualifications (SQ) or technical qualifications (DQ) that you could be trained for?

A. Assault Engineers, Armourer, Aircrewman, Chef, Clerk, Drill Leader, Driver, Electronic Warfare, Heavy Weapons - Air Defence/Anti-tank/Mortars, Illustrator, Landing Craft, General Duties, Medical Assistant, Metal Smith, Military Provost, Mountain Leader, PTI, Platoon Weapons, Signals, Stores, Accountant, Swimmer Canoeist, Telecommunication Tech, Vehicle Mechanic.

Q24. How long do you sign on for when joining the Royal Marines?

A. 22 years open engagement.

Q25. What is the minimum return of service that you have to give as a Royal Marine?

A. 4 Years.

Q. What is the name of the current rifle in use with the Royal Marines?

A. SA80 A2 / 5.56mm Assault Rifle

Q26. How many weeks training do you undergo to become a Royal Marine?

A. 30 weeks

Q27. What is the role of assault ships with regard to the Royal Marines?

A. To carry an Embarked Military Force, which includes landing craft, helicopters and troops, and to provide naval artillery for landings.

Q28. Give the names of the assault ships in the Royal Navy?

A. HMS Ocean, HMS Albion and HMS Bulwark.

Q29. Where is the headquarters of the Royal Marines situated?

A. Whale Island, Portsmouth.

Q30. Name two types of vehicles used by the Royal Marines.

A. Landing Craft Utility - (LCUs)

Landing Craft Air Cushion (Light) - (LCAC (L))

Rigid Raiding Craft - (RRC)

Inflatable Raiding Craft - (IRC Mk2)

Helicopters - Lynx & Chinook

Q31. List the Rank structure in the Royal Marines from Marine to Warrant Officer.

A. Marine, Lance Corporal, Corporal, Sergeant, Colour Sergeant, W02, W01

Q32. List the rank structure from Captain to Major General.

A. Captain, Major, Colonel, Brigadier, Major General.

Q33. Where in the world do the Royal Marines carry out their Arctic Training?

A. Norway.

Q34. How does a Royal Marine earn the coveted Green Beret?

A. By completing the Commando course, which includes:

- The Endurance Course in 72 mins;

- Tarzan Assault Course in 13 mins;

- 9-Mile Speed March in 90 mins;

- 30 mile in 8 hrs;

And also demonstrating the Commando qualities.

TOP INTERVIEW TIPS

- When you walk into the interview room stand up straight with your shoulders back.

- Project an image of confidence but do not be over-confident, cocky or arrogant.

- Don't sit down in the interview chair until invited to do so.

- Sit with your hands resting on your knees, palms downwards. It is ok to use your hands expressively but don't overdo it.

- Address the interviewer as Sir or Ma'am.

- Don't slouch in the chair.

- Speak up and be positive.

- Be smart and take a pride in your appearance. Wear a suit or a shirt and tie at the very least.

- Make sure you have researched both the Royal Marines and your chosen branch.

- Go the extra mile and learn a little bit about the Royal Marines history. When the panel ask you 'What can you tell us about the Royal Marines?' you will be able to demonstrate that you have made an effort to look into their history as well as their modern day activities.

- Be respectful and courteous towards the interview panel.

- Ask positive questions at the end of the interview. Try not to ask questions such as "How much leave will I get?" or "How often do I get paid?" Questions I would recommend you ask are:

    Q. If I am successful, how long would it be before I start?

    Q. Can you recommend any specific areas that I need to work on in order to improve?

- If unsure about a question try not to 'waffle'. If you do not know the answer then it is okay to say so. Move on to the next question and put it behind you.

- Finally, believe in yourself and be confident.

CHAPTER 9
PREPARING FOR THE PRMC

INTRODUCTION

The Potential Royal Marines Course (PRMC) is a 2½ day test of your suitability for becoming a Royal Marines Commando. As you can imagine, it is very hard to pass. However, if you approach it in the right manner, both mentally and physically, then you can pass with flying colours. It is important to remember that the Royal Marines are not looking for the finished article during the PRMC, which is why the title of the course starts off with 'potential'. 'Potential' is exactly what they are looking for from candidates during the 2½ day PRMC. Show them that you have the potential, and they will turn you into one of the most feared and respected soldiers in the world.

MENTAL ABILITY

Cast your mind back to the beginning of this guide, when I

wrote about the Royal Marines that I know, and have worked with, during my career. Their ability to do just about anything came from their mental approach, as well as their all-round physical ability too. Commandos are not 'meat heads' who can lift heavy weights down the gym for hours on end. Yes, they are physically strong, but they are also mentally strong too, which is what you will need to be if you are to pass PRMC. Also, cast your mind back to the beginning of the guide when I wrote about the firefighter physical tests that I went through when I was joining the Fire Service. Remember the hose running test and how shattered I was? Remember that physically, I couldn't go any further, but mentally I was prepared to. I could have given up at that point, but I chose not to. Even though I couldn't move another inch, or carry another length of hose, I passed, simply because I chose not to give in. It is this state of mind that will get you through PRMC. Learn to apply this state of mind and attitude at any given moment, and it is a skill that will serve you well, not only during your career in the Royal Marines, but also during your life as a whole – never give up!

PHYSICAL ABILITY

I believe this is the easy part. It is totally down to you to get yourself fit enough to pass PRMC. When I say pass, I don't mean pass by the skin of your teeth, but rather pass with flying colours.

Let's take the multi-stage fitness test (bleep test) for example. What level can you achieve right now? I believe the multi-stage fitness test is one of the most effective ways of building up cardiovascular fitness. At the time of writing this guide I still run five miles, five times a week. For a bloke who's fast approaching 40, that's not a bad fitness regime! The last time

I did the multi-stage fitness I was approximately 30 years old, and I smashed level 14 with ease. There is no excuse for not getting yourself a copy of the test and practising it 3 or 4 times a week. Your fitness levels will improve rapidly and, if you mix it in with some long endurance runs and gym work, you will soon be well above the 'potential' level that you are trying to achieve during your preparation.

You do not need to carry out any advanced type of exercise during your preparation for the PRMC. All you need to carry out are:

- Press-ups

- Sit-ups

- Pull-ups (heaves)

- Multi-stage fitness test

- Long distance endurance runs

- Swimming and treading water

Implement the above exercises into your daily routine and you'll have a far greater chance of succeeding at the PRMC.

WHAT DOES THE PRMC CONSIST OF?

The Potential Royal Marines Course (PRMC) is a 2½ day-long residential selection event that is used to assess, as it says, your 'potential' to become a Royal Marine. The PRMC is held at the Commando Training Centre Royal Marines (CTCRM), which is located near to Exmouth. During this 2½ day course you will be given the opportunity to show the recruitment staff that you have what it takes to join this elite service. It is important that you remember that it is down to you to prove that you have the potential to become a Royal

Marine. Don't go there unprepared but instead do everything in your power to improve your chances of success.

During the PRMC the Royal Marines will be looking to see that you have the determination, physical fitness, stamina, mental ability, cool headedness and the ability to rise to a challenge. Demonstrating all of these is a tall order but there are lots of things you can do to improve your chances. Later on in this section of the guide we will look at the ways you can achieve this. To begin with let's take a look at what you will go through during the PRMC.

THE PRMC TIMETABLE

When you receive your joining instructions for the PRMC it will provide you with detailed information about the course, what you need to take with you and how to prepare for it. As with all recruitment literature you should read it carefully and the follow the instructions as directed. There is no doubt about it; the PRMC will be hard. 99% of people who attend the PRMC find it extremely difficult but the main thing is not to give up. Remember one of the key qualities they are looking for is determination! Be prepared to do many sit-ups and press-ups during your stay at the PRMC.

When you arrive at the PRMC you will be met straight away by the Duty Instructor. As soon as you get off the train he will be waiting for you. He will take a roll call before briefing you on your next movements. Remember to listen to everything he tells you. You are being assessed right from the word go and you must be able to follow his instructions to the letter. I recommend that you attend the PRMC wearing a smart formal outfit. I would advise against jeans, t-shirts and trainers. Make sure your shoes are polished, don't put your hands in your pockets, stand up straight and do not fidget.

Following registration you will be able to meet the other candidates at PRMC and generally settle in. You will be issued with your kit, which you will be expected to wear during your stay at the PRMC and also receive a briefing on what you will go through during the course. Again, it is important that you listen carefully to everything that you are being told.

Once you have been fully briefed you will have the opportunity to eat. Whilst it's important to eat a good nutritional meal, remember that you'll be carrying out plenty of exercises during the following two days. Eat foods that are guaranteed to provide you with plenty of carbohydrates and fuel. I also recommend that you drink plenty of water in order to prevent dehydration, and also to maintain concentration levels.

During the first day you may also be required to sit a basic Maths and Literacy test. If you are concerned about these tests then I recommend you try the online psychometric testing facility available at www.how2become.co.uk.

THE PRMC TIMETABLE – DAY 1

Your first full day will involve many activities and you will not have a minute to yourself. The day will begin at 6am, when you will have to get up, get showered, shaved, dressed and clean the room before going for breakfast. Your definition of a clean and tidy bedroom will probably be different to that of a Royal Marines Commando. However, they will soon let you know if the room isn't clean and tidy! After a briefing from the Course Director you will take your first gym test.

GYM TEST 1

Gym test 1 consists of the following assessments:

- A 3-mile run that is divided up into two parts. The first part is a 1.5-mile run that is undertaken as part of a squad. This must be completed in a time of 12 minutes 30 seconds. The second part is a 1.5-mile run that is conducted on your own, and as a 'best effort' timed run. You must complete this as quickly as possible. Anyone who takes longer than 10 minutes 30 seconds will fail the course.

During the squad element of the run I advise that you support other team members and encourage the weaker ones. Remember that you are running as part of a squad and they will be assessing not only your fitness, but your team working ability also.

During the second element of the run, which is the best effort 1.5 miler, you must go all out to complete it within your fastest time possible. Note the word 'effort'. They are looking for 110% during this run and you should be easily capable of completing it within a time of fewer than ten minutes.

- Multi-stage fitness test. You are required to reach level 13 during this part of the test, which is usually carried out during the afternoon of the first full day.

- Press-ups. You will be required to perform 60 continuous press-ups within 2 minutes using the correct technique. The correct technique involves keeping the body straight at all times. You will need to lower your chest down to meet another candidate's fist. When you return back to the starting position you will need to fully lock out your arms. Your hands should be shoulder width apart and your elbows must be kept into your sides.

- Sit-ups. You will be required to perform 80 continuous sits-ups within 2 minutes, again using the correct

technique. The correct technique involves your feet being held down by another candidate. Your fingers must stay in contact with the sides of your head and your elbows must make contact with the mat on the downward motion. On the upward motion your elbows must come up to touch the knees, which must be kept together throughout the duration of the exercise.

• Pull-ups. You will be required to perform 6 pull-ups using an overhand grip. Your body will hang straight whilst holding on to a wooden beam. You must pull yourself up until your chin is over the beam. This exercise is carried out to the commands of "bend and stretch", which is used to ensure discipline during the exercise and also prevent you from using swinging motions to pull yourself up. You must keep in time with the commands.

HOW TO PREPARE FOR GYM TEST 1

• Start getting up at 6am every morning and go out on a 3-mile run. This will not only get you into the right frame of mind for early starts, but it will also start to prepare you for your initial Royal Marines training, where early starts are the norm! At least one of your weekly 3-mile runs should be on a 'best effort' basis. Although you are only required to perform a 1.5-mile run best effort during the first day, by carrying out a 3-mile best effort you will greatly increase your ability for the real test.

• Get a copy of the bleep test and start practising it, at least three times a week. Before you attend PRMC I recommend that you try to reach level 14 as an absolute minimum. The bleep test is performed over a 20-metre course and involves you running backwards and forwards to a timed 'bleep'. The actual test goes up to 23 levels

but not many people can achieve this. The test itself can be obtained by visiting our website: www.how2become.co.uk.

- I recommend that you are capable of carrying out at least 10 continuous effective pull-ups before you attend PRMC. Pull-ups are probably one of the hardest exercises to execute, simply because you have to lift your own body weight. The unfortunate thing about this type of exercise is that you will probably need to attend a gym in order to carry them out. Having said that, there are a number of different types of 'pull-up bars' available to buy on the market that can be easily and safely fitted to a doorway at home. If you choose to purchase one of these items, make sure that it conforms to the relevant safety standards first. During the PRMC you will be required to perform 6 pull-ups during the test, but aim to be capable of carrying out at least 10 before PRMC. The pull-ups will need to be performed with your palms facing away from you. These are considerably harder to perform than with your palms facing towards you. Therefore, you will need to practise harder. During your practise do not use any form of swinging motion. Your exercises should be disciplined, strict and use only your isolated upper body strength to correctly execute the pull-up.

- Be capable of carrying out at least 60 correctly executed press-ups and 80 sit-ups before you attend PRMC. This can easily be achieved by performing the exercises on a daily basis, and gradually increasing the number over a prolonged period of time. Remember that you will need to carry these out within a 2-minute time period during PRMC, so practise accordingly.

ASSAULT COURSE

This will test your ability to the limit. This is basically an assault course assessment, which assesses your strength, stamina, height capability and determination. When tackling the course you will have to climb walls, ropes, climbing frames, tunnels and water troughs to name just a few. The assault course element will go on for at least 2.5 hours! Therefore you will need to posses a great deal of stamina to complete it and impress the instructors.

Before you do the assault course you will go through a warm-up stage with the instructors. This will include press-ups, sit-ups, running around and anything else that they can think of in order to wear you down. This means that when you come to do the assault course you will already be tired. However, remember that the instructors are looking for determination. Whatever you do, do not give up. Even if you are on your last legs it is vitally important that you keep going, even if you cannot move any further. This sounds contradictory, but the instructors are looking for you to demonstrate the determination to succeed and complete the course even when you are shattered. Remember the firefighter fitness test that I went through? Keep reminding yourself that you must not give in whatever happens.

Although this element of the course is entitled the 'assault course', it is actually split up into 3 different elements as follows:

High obstacle course
This course will assess your ability to work at height. You will have to climb ladders, traverse ropes and negotiate obstacles at heights up to a maximum of 30 feet from the ground.

Assault course

The assault course element is a 'best effort' performance. The instructors will demonstrate the correct techniques to get round the course before giving you the opportunity to show them what you can do.

Endurance course

The endurance course is extremely tough. Not only does it come at the end of the assault course assessment, but it will also last for approximately 60 minutes. The course itself is primarily designed to assess your determination, commitment and resolve. Remember how we have covered the important subject of 'mindset'? Well now's your chance to put it into practice.

The endurance course includes shuttle sprints, being fully immersed in water, press-ups, upper body exercises and running. The key to passing this element of the course is not to give in, however tired you feel. You will be watched closely and assessed to see if you can operate effectively whilst pushing yourself to the limit.

SWIMMING ASSESSMENT

Once you have completed the first gym test you will be taken to the swimming pool for an assessment. The aim of this test is to jump into a swimming pool from a diving board and then swim a length of the pool using breaststroke. This is a relatively simple test and one that will not need too much preparation. However, it is worthwhile taking into consideration that swimming is a fantastic way to improve your overall fitness and stamina. I strongly advise that you incorporate swimming sessions into your preparation plan. If you cannot currently swim then I advise that you go down to your local pool and get yourself some lessons. Breaststroke

is relatively easy to learn and it is also a great way to cross train and improve your cardiovascular fitness.

COMMANDO SLIDE

During this assessment you will be strapped into a safety harness so there is no need to worry, although you will need to be comfortable with heights to pass the assessment. Basically you will then, as the title suggests, slide down a long wire until you reach the bottom.

INTERVIEW

You will be interviewed during the PRMC on your motivations for wanting to become a Royal Marines Commando. Whilst a large proportion of your preparation time will be spent on the physical aspect of the course, you must not neglect the interview stage. All you need to do is read all of your recruitment literature; visit the Royal Marines website at royalnavy.mod.uk, and visit online chat forums that will allow you to communicate with other candidates who have been through selection. Online forums will also allow you the opportunity to ask serving Royal Marines specific questions that relate to selection and PRMC.

PASSING PRMC

Surprisingly, not that many people fail PRMC. However, many people do withdraw from PRMC before they reach the end. There will certainly be times when you feel like giving up, but the important thing is to keep going regardless.

If you reach the end of the course then there is a strong possibility that you will be offered a Recruit Troop joining

date, usually not far off in the future. If you fail PRMC then you may be offered the opportunity to return to try again in the future.

FINAL TIPS FOR PASSING THE PRMC

• The majority of people who fail the PRMC do so during the 3-mile run. Even though this is the first assessment, candidates are not aware that if they fail to achieve the required grade, they will fail the entire PRMC. It is crucial that you can achieve the second part, the 1.5-mile run best effort, in less than 10 minutes.

• Don't spend hours in the gym in the build up to PRMC. Instead, concentrate on your running, bleep test ability, sit-ups, press-ups, pull-ups and a little bit of swimming. You can pass PRMC without the need to attend a gym.

• Always aim for a higher standard during your preparation. Don't be content with the minimum. Remember – train hard, race easy!

A FEW FINAL WORDS

You have now reached the end of the guide and will no doubt brimming with confidence and enthusiasm at what lies ahead of you. Anything in life that is worth having, such as a career with the Royal Marines, is worth working hard for. The selection process is not easy. In fact, I personally believe that it is one of the most difficult selection processes of any of the worldwide armed forces. However, if you approach your preparation with the right vigour and mental attitude then you will be able to pass it.

Don't leave your preparation to the last couple of weeks leading up to PRMC. Start working well in advance of your application and spend at least 75% of your preparation time working on your physical fitness. Don't spend hours in the gym, but instead work on the basic exercises that I have covered in this guide. Whilst performing pull-ups, sit-ups and press-ups, work hard on your technique – this will make your job a lot easier during PRMC.

Finally, it is crucial that you believe in yourself. You must have the confidence and determination not only to pass the selection process, but also to prepare hard for it. Remember that each time you push yourself harder during your preparation, you will be taking one step further towards becoming a Commando.

Work hard, stay focused and be what you want…

Best wishes,

Richard McMunn

Visit www.how2become.co.uk to find more titles and courses that will help you to pass the Royal Marines Commando selection process, including:

- How to pass the Royal Marines interview DVD.

- 1 Day Royal Marines Officer training course.

- Psychometric testing books and CD's.

www.how2become.co.uk